PENGUIN BOOKS

TAX SHELTERS IN PLAIN ENGLISH

Robert Daniel Fierro has been on the "tax shelter trail" since these investments began coming out of the woodwork into the light of public scrutiny in 1970. As a journalist, commentator, and consultant, he has written, lectured, and advised about these controversial investments, gleaning knowledge as an insider and offering opinions to both the consumer and organizer. Author of scores of magazine, newsletter, and newspaper articles on tax shelters and other aspects of personal finance, Mr. Fierro was an editor of the famed *McGraw-Hill's Personal Finance Letter*. His articles have also appeared in *The New York Times*, *Barron's*, *Money*, *Venture*, *Travel & Leisure*, investment newsletters, and other specialized publications. He has appeared on radio and television programs about tax shelters and operates a Thoroughbred racing and breeding consulting firm from his base of operations in Whitestone, New York.

TAX SHELTERS
IN PLAIN ENGLISH

New Strategies for the 1980s

Revised and Updated Edition

by

ROBERT DANIEL FIERRO

PENGUIN BOOKS

Penguin Books Ltd, Harmondsworth,
Middlesex, England
Penguin Books, 625 Madison Avenue,
New York, New York 10022, U.S.A.
Penguin Books Australia Ltd, Ringwood,
Victoria, Australia
Penguin Books Canada Limited, 2801 John Street,
Markham, Ontario, Canada L3R 1B4
Penguin Books (N.Z.) Ltd, 182–190 Wairau Road,
Auckland 10, New Zealand

First published in the United States of America by
Farnsworth Publishing Company, Inc., 1981
Revised Edition published in Penguin Books 1983
Reprinted 1984

LIBRARY OF CONGRESS CATALOGING IN PUBLICATION DATA
Fierro, Robert Daniel.
    Tax shelters in plain English.
    Includes index.
    1. Tax shelters—Law and legislation—
United States.   I. Title.
KF6297.5.Z9F53   1982   343.7305'23   82-7543
ISBN 0 14 00.6362 5   347.303523   AACR2

Printed in the United States of America by
R. R. Donnelley & Sons Company, Harrisonburg, Virginia
Set in English Times

Portions of this book have appeared in various form
in *McGraw-Hill's Personal Finance Letter, Pan Am
Clipper, Prime Time,* and *Venture: The Magazine for
Entrepreneurs.*

This book is dedicated to the memory of David A. Gracer, whose integrity and love for life continue to provide inspiration.

Contents

Acknowledgments

Journalists have this habit of actually believing what they write is the product of their own imagination and knowledge. In truth, we do imagine a great deal (as our media are sometimes prone to reveal) but we don't know too much—especially if we went to journalism school. "We have to be carefully taught," in the words of Oscar Hammerstein, and when it comes to this book, I have had some extraordinary teachers. Some of these people, to be sure, are not exactly what you would call good examples of the industry they represent. Yet, one can learn a great deal from the charlatan as well as from the prudent. To all the charlatans who've crossed my path during the past decade, I thank you for your help.

To the prudent, most of whom are mentioned in the following pages, goes my sincere appreciation for putting up with my dumbness and opinions over the years. In particular, I'd like to give special thanks to Philip Strassler, CPA, for his kind remarks and comments on this manuscript, and for his encouragement. My own accountant, Jerry Berg, hates to see his name in print, but I simply had to get back at him after all these years, so, thanks, Jerry.

In addition, I would like to thank the people at McGraw-Hill's Newsletter Center for their encouragement regarding the first edition of this book, most especially George Lutjen. Of course, my agent, Felicia Eth, comes in for praise, if only for putting up with and sticking by me. A special acknowledgment as well to editors such as Bayard Hooper, Ruth Kelton, Sharon Pavlista, Carl Burgen, Dee Wedemeyer, and Roger

Harris for assigning the kinds of articles which helped me hone my ideas, and gather some of my facts. And for his remarkable faith and kindness, and inspiration, thank you Andy Tobias.

The only other person I think I should thank is my charming wife, Alice Victoria Bernadette; but if I did, she'd get suspicious.

Introduction:
What Is ERTA
If Not A Mass-
Transit System?

I am not one to quibble with history, but the plain fact of the matter is that in the past dozen years there have been four successive major pieces of tax legislation which, in their initial stages at least, were aimed at "reforming" the ways in which government siphons money from the citizenry.

And not one of them reformed a damn thing.

Instead, beginning with the neo-socialistic Tax Reform Act of 1969, proceeding with some momentum through the transitional liberal Tax Reform Act of 1976, segueing to the pendulum-swinging Revenue Act of 1978, and culminating with the neo-Neanderthal Economic Recovery Tax Act of 1981 (ERTA), these various laws have only served to create new opportunities for certain people to build major industries at the expense of the government.

This should give us some insight into our national character: We dearly love to say that we're socking it to the rich, but secretly, we're setting things up so that when we get rich, the government won't take it away from us.

It's called Winning Is The Only Thing.

How odd, then, that these great industries, which have mushroomed from the minds of entrepreneurs, accountants, attorneys, and assorted biological freaks from Wall Street, should be structured on the principle of *losing*. Even the generic name given to these industries collectively—tax *shelters*—suggests a retreat of sorts. Definitely against the national character, the kind of stuff to make Custer spin in his dusty grave.

But then, it would also be in our character if, in spinning, old George should happen to strike oil; his ghost wouldn't mind it one bit if his descendants wrote off on their tax returns the labor George expended as an "intangible drilling expense," and then applied for a 25% investment tax credit for transforming a historic site (Custer's grave) into a condo.

Such is the way the wonderful world of tax shelters works. It's often a hilarious world, populated by some of the biggest jokers in the history of capitalism, but it's a serious world as well. Few people understand that it was partly because the American economy was so flexible as to allow tax shelters to prosper that certain things happened that many overlook in their criticism of these investments. For one thing, a lot of jobs were created in many industries—energy, real estate, farming, equipment leasing, finance—through the real infusion of capital that good investments with tax shelter aspects can bring. Tax shelters have played an important role in the economy over the past dozen or so years, and they're likely to continue to do so for many years to come. They are simply acceptable to too many people who vote. Like you.

Unfortunately, tax shelters have also produced thieves and twits. The thieves have been with us since the days of Ali Baba. The twits are the investors. It constantly amazes me how many "sophisticated investors" are willing to throw their money at slickly dressed, fast-talking snake-oil salesmen—all in the name of beating Uncle Sam. If you happen to be one of them, this book will be a mirror to your past.

If you are new to the game of tax shelters, this book will be your guide. We spare few reputations herein, including that of the author, I'm afraid, and this is mercifully not what you would call a technical book. Neither, however, do we hope to be too glib—although a dozen years on this beat can lead to a bit of cynicism, perhaps.

There are major problems with writing a book about tax shelters: after all, every four years it would tend to become obsolete. However, what changes is only the numbers—and those have been altered since this book was first published in 1981 because of the Economic Recovery Tax Act, hereinafter referred to as ERTA. (Sounds like a mass transit system, doesn't it?) What should never change, however, is your *attitude*, and you're going to get plenty of that in this book.

One or two tax shelters have been adversely affected by ERTA: government-sponsored housing and commodity straddles come readily to mind. Others have been given avaricious boosts: equipment leasing, certain kinds of real estate, aspects of farming, for example. No doubt at this minute someone is attempting to create a whole new industry out of the loopholes opened by ERTA—one to rival such fabled ventures as abalone farming, Bible peddling, master record cutting, and signed lithographs by failed living artists. Through it all, the rules remain the same.

This book will give you the rules, and maybe a few chuckles along the way.

Part One

"What Is A Tax Shelter— And Why Is My Stockbroker Trying To Sell Me One Of These Things?"

1.

"The Hell With Death And Taxes . . . Gimme Shelter!"

Say what you will about inflation, the fact remains that it's given a great many Americans a rather accelerated, if not queasy, view of life from the upper income tax brackets. The financial vertigo induced by seeing one's tax bill these days can be treated with various investment remedies, of course. Unfortunately, too often what results is an even worse case of the financial vapors—i.e., your money continues to disappear, poof! into the pocket of some promoter, if not down some forsaken hole in the ground on Alaska's *South* Slope.

I don't care what you've heard about how much taxes are coming down as a result of ERTA, the fact remains that a whole lot of Americans are going to be stuck paying hefty tax bills at least through 1984, when the tax rates change dramatically. By then, however, the effects of inflation will probably have gotten totally out of hand, and we'll all be able to afford fine bone china place settings for 200 people, to say nothing about salivating after tax shelter. Until then, you'll still be paying relatively through the nose if you're in any of the "marginal tax brackets."

What we are talking about is tax shelters, America's most misunderstood, controversial, explosively growing, and sexy way of making or losing money. Only in America, it seems, does there exist a tax structure so wondrously chaotic in philosophy as to go completely against the psyche of the people it serves. For when it comes to tax shelters, you can sum up the entire topic with a simple twist of Vince Lombardi's most immortalized phrase:

Losing isn't everything; it's the *only* thing.

It's a little bit of national madness, this business about tax shelters. Every April 15th, or thereabouts, just as we are harboring revolutionary thoughts, the media rub salt in our wounds by trotting out tales of how many millionaires pay little or no taxes—because of loopholes in the Tax Code. This was hard enough to swallow when there was a clear difference between the millionaire set and the rest of us slobs who could be conveniently classified as upper-middle-class or, egad, even middle-class taxpayers. Ah, the Good Old Days—like up until 1978 or so—when inflation and an antiquated tax bracket structure began pushing a lot more of us into the same tax situations as those cursed millionaires.

Philip Strassler, a New York City CPA, mused on this topic one day with me. His numbers, however, were *not* amusing. "It doesn't take a whole lot of *taxable* income before you start paying 49% of it to the government," he said. If you're single, you start paying through the nose at the $41,500 mark; joint filers fare only mildly better, hitting the charmed circle at $60,000. This means that a salaried single person earning from $50,000 to $60,000 per year, and a two-income family with joint salaries of as little as $70,000 could now qualify as "millionaires" in this country, tax shelterwise, at least.

Middle class, indeed.

Michael Convissar of Kenneth Leventhal & Company, CPAs, New York City, summed up the situation neatly, if not gruesomely: "These people are not generating a heck of a lot of cash—but they are generating a *lot* of tax."

Amen, brothers and sisters, and that is why you've purchased this book, which is, of course, tax-deductible. We are going to discuss tax shelters in a way which will hopefully give you something profound to say at the next party you attend—or meeting you have with your accountant or stockbroker. We will do this in a manner which will go easy on the mumbo jumbo, and will come down hard on the side of plain common sense. By the time you're through reading this book, you will not only be able to understand tax shelters, but you will also be conversant on the matter. This will lead to two immediate results:

(1) You will become a much-sought-after party guest, possibly making the "A list," if you're flamboyant enough.

(2) You will not make any dumb moves to cut your taxes. You will be able to plan intelligently, analyze

Here are the new tax rate schedules as a result of ERTA, and how they'll be phased in over the next few years:

SINGLE INDIVIDUALS

Taxable Income	1982 Pay + % on Excess	1983 Pay + % on Excess	1984 Pay + % on Excess
$ 34,100 - $ 41,500	$ 8,812 + 44%	$ 7,953 + 40%	$ 7,507 + 38%
41,500 - 55,300	12,068 + 50%	10,913 + 45%	10,319 + 42%
55,300 - 81,800	18,968 + 50%	17,123 + 50%	16,115 + 48%
81,800 - 108,300	32,218 + 50%	30,373 + 50%	28,835 + 50%
108,300 - upward	45,468 + 50%	43,623 + 50%	42,085 + 50%

MARRIED FILING JOINTLY, OR SURVIVING SPOUSE

Taxable Income	1982 Pay + % on Excess	1983 Pay + % on Excess	1984 Pay + % on Excess
$ 45,800 - $ 60,000	$11,457 + 44%	$10,334 + 40%	$ 9,772 + 38%
60,000 - 85,600	17,705 + 49%	16,014 + 44%	15,168 + 42%
85,600 - 109,400	30,249 + 50%	27,278 + 48%	29,920 + 45%
109,400 - 162,400	42,149 + 50%	38,702 + 50%	36,930 + 49%
162,400 - 251,400	68,649 + 50%	65,202 + 50%	62,600 + 50%
215,400 - upward	95,149 + 50%	91,702 + 50%	89,100 + 50%

given opportunities, and allocate your financial resources in ways which will not leave gaping holes either on your balance sheet, or in your wallet.

Mercifully, there will be very little technical talk, and precious few charts and forms to cross your eyes. The technicalities are readily translatable into plain English; and the paperwork you should leave to your tax advisor. (If you don't have one of the latter, you're already not as terribly bright as you think.)

But, read on. And, trust me. I've been hanging around tax shelters for more than a decade now, sticking my nose into some of the most unlikely places, and discussing the topic with quite an odd assortment of characters. Some of these people, and experiences, you will meet on these pages. They will help tell our tale of how the tax-shelter industry grew up during the 1970s and 1980s by taking advantage of greed, inflation, fear, and the tax laws, to a point where it's now the glamour boy of Wall Street, the nemesis of the Internal Revenue Service, and the wolf-in-sheep's clothing for the investment public.

Through it all, you will be fascinated by the concepts, titillated by the possibilities, and lectured about the pitfalls involved. We will spare no reputation, but we will also not downplay the potential for true financial satisfaction, either.

Yes, you *can* cut taxes and make money by investing in tax shelters. But you must understand at the outset that regardless of what anyone tells you—promoter, broker, press, golfing buddy, or brother-in-law—there is absolutely no free lunch involved. This book is merely designed to prevent indigestion.

2.

Get Thy
Act Together

Planning is its own reward, as the Management-by-Objectives gurus are wont to say. Yet it's a source of wonderment to discover how many intelligent people treat their financial—and by extension tax—situations from the seat of their pants or hem of their skirts. What's more surprising is the widespread belief that very little can be done to reduce one's taxes well in advance of the Ides of April without running afoul of the law, or adrift of the cash flow.

Look, the Tax Code *runs* this country. It's so chock-full of loopholes because the capitalist system feeds on the element of risk. Our government provides protection for the system through a unique application of the car-rot/stick philosophy: If you're willing to take a financial risk for the sake of the national well-being, the government will tax you less.

You want to help the poor or afflicted? Contribute to charity, and deduct the amount from your gross income, thereby reducing your own tax base. You want to help stabilize your community? Buy a house and finance it with a loan from a local bank. You get to deduct the interest on the mortgage, and the bank makes enough of a profit to relend the money to small businesses or local residents for other home purchases, or financing of capital goods.

You should not feel guilty, therefore, if you harbor thoughts about getting into a tax shelter, for Congress has written tax laws providing you with the options to act on those thoughts. You *should* feel guilty, however, if you decide to exercise that option at the last legal minute, without thinking about your predicament until November or December of the taxable year involved. In that case, you get what you deserve—a probable screwing, and perhaps an audit.

The first thing to keep in mind about tax shelter investments is that you should try to avoid them at all costs if you are in the "marginal" Federal income tax brackets. These range from the point where your taxable income (after all common deductions) is taxed at rates between 33% and 49%. In dollar figures, that amounts to taxable income of as little as $18,200 for the single taxpayer, and $24,600 for the joint filers, according to Phil Strassler.

There are two sound reasons for avoiding tax shelters at these income levels:

1. There are a variety of safer options open to people in the middle tax brackets which do not require high risk or substantial amounts of cash investment.

2. The numbers just don't work out to your advantage.

Let's look at Reason #1 for a while. (Reason #2 will be explained in Chapter Three.) If you're making enough money to be thrown into the middle brackets, wise planning and nonfrivolous spending habits should enable you to cut your tax bill enough each year so that your taxable income might fall below the 33% level. While this may still seem somewhat painful, remember that most of the 33% is taken through withholding. It may be depressing to look at your deflated paycheck in that light, but recognize that you do have to pay a share of your income to keep the country rolling along (to prosperity, or oblivion, depending on your politics). In addition, if you plan properly, you'll most likely qualify for some kind of refund, which most people use to pay for vacations designed to bolster the economics of other nations.

There are steps you can take, alone or with the help of a good financial advisor, to keep your tax bill smaller than you expected—even if you go over the magic 49% mark.

You can begin to get your act together under the guidance of a good advisor, or a small team of same. This doesn't mean your Uncle Charlie who does taxes on the side, or one of your buddies who's an insurance agent at heart by day and dabbles in financial advice at night. No, there are only three kinds of financial advisors you should seek out to help you get a handle on your tax planning: a tax attorney, a Certified Public Accountant (CPA), or a qualified personal financial planner. The CPA is absolutely essential; the other two are optional, depending upon your situation.

Tax attorneys are the gold miners of the financial world. As such their services are usually very expensive, and their talents are best utilized by those who can afford the high stakes involved in mining all the crevices of the Tax Code. Generally speaking, tax attorneys work for the true millionaires, arranging their affairs and seeking out—or organizing—deals which are designed to maximize one's opportunity for real profit while minimizing tax exposure on the way in, and out. These folks often are cross-licensed in accounting, usually having gone as far as becoming CPAs.

Entrepreneurs with delusions of grandeur, high-priced performing artists and athletes, the aggressive landed gentry—these are the kinds of folks who most often hook up with tax attorneys. Companies are purchased or created; promotions and product endorsements arranged; farms and professional sports clubs are gobbled up in whole or in part; airplanes leased, coal mines captured, oil and gas wells drilled or purchased, office and industrial parks constructed—deals conceived, structured, and closed primarily by tax attorneys on a semi-discretionary basis. In other words, tax attorneys have a good deal of say in running the total business lives of their clients. Thus, their services appeal to but a handful of people. But they usually call upon the adjunct services of a good CPA as well.

When we talk about the accounting profession in this country, we tend to lump all practitioners under one common heading: Accountant. That's all very good for journalists who have to save space, but for your purposes, the only kind of accountant you should seek to help with tax planning is a *Certified* Public Accountant —most especially, one whose specialty is individual tax situations. There are simply too many areas other than personal taxes where accountants are involved these days for one to assume that all accountants—even all CPAs—are tax mavens. If you happen to own your own business, you'll definitely want a CPA who is skilled in all the tax nuances of sole proprietorships or closely held companies as well; as a bonus, these people are also expert in maximizing your personal cash flow and minimizing your tax bite.

There are a few ways of going about selecting a good CPA, but I prefer the advice of financial writer David W. Kennedy of New York City, who makes a number of commonsense recommendations.

"You should start by getting suggestions of friends, colleagues, or relatives who you think are in the same tax or financial situation that you're in," says Kennedy. "Then you'll have to do a bit of interviewing." Be prepared to do this even if you currently have a CPA with whom you're not totally thrilled, whether for professional or personal reasons. It could very well be that your CPA is with a firm which is too large to consider your return very profitable. It may be time to seek out a smaller, aggressive firm. If you're really in a bind, say through a sudden increase in salary or through inheritance or windfall profit, you might also want to look for a CPA whose specialty is tax deferral as well as tax shelter, or who might be a tax attorney to boot. Remember, of course, that the more parchment on the wall, the higher the fee you'll pay— which is at least tax deductible.

Perhaps the most important criterion you'll be looking for in a CPA is the ability to plan tax strategy carefully. Many CPAs are very reluctant, however, to become involved in recommending any kind of investment action which will reduce your taxes—either generic or specific. If you find a CPA in this category whom you like, don't disqualify him or her from the job if you encounter this reluctance. There are other people who can be added to your team, and we'll meet a few of them shortly.

Meanwhile, Dave Kennedy suggests you keep the following five points in mind when you look for a good CPA:

1. You'll want to know if the CPA's past experience is compatible with your problems. Ask for the names of two or three present—and past—clients to determine whether they were happy with recent services rendered. Discuss some of your financial problems—poor cash flow, heavy year-end tax load, periodic untaxed bonuses or commissions—to get a feel as to how the CPA will steer you.

2. Get a handle on the CPA's current knowledge of the field of taxation and the moves within the IRS to tighten the screws on people like you. Ask which professional journals he or she reads, and whether he or she subscribes to the *IRS Cumulative Bulletin,* which is where all the rulings, interpretations, and smoke signals from the boys and girls in Washington, D.C., first appear. Ask to see a copy of the *Bulletin,* and have the CPA explain one of the rulings to you. You may also want to inquire whether the CPA is continuing his or her education by attending refresher courses or seminars on personal taxation.

3. Has the CPA represented clients before the IRS during an audit or challenge, and how have they fared? Ask how high in the challenge procedure the CPA has gone—simply an audit, or through the Tax Courts. What were the results—and who got the credit, or blame?

Remember, however, that a CPA with too much experience in the Tax Courts may be a bit too creative for you.

4. Ask whether your return will be processed by hand or computer. Now, I'm not too thrilled with the prospect of turning my receipts over to a machine, but understand that these days CPAs can be far more productive getting your tax situation in line with the help of a computer. That's because the machine does all the calculations, while the human mind tackles the creative options. You will also discover that a CPA who's hooked into a computer may cost less, since CPAs generally share time on a computer. This cuts down on expenses by eliminating the need for the CPA to figure everything out by hand, which takes longer. At $25 to $100 per hour for human time, the use of a computer can save you some cash.

5. Just to calm your nerves, suggest some outrageous deduction to the prospective CPA, and wait for the reaction. You might, for example, suggest a totally ridiculous casualty loss, or try to charge your vacation off as a business expense. The kind of CPA you want will ask for documented proof of these alleged deductions, and will not let you get away with anything which might kick up a red flag in the IRS computer. The CPA's name goes on the tax return as well as yours, so he or she is putting something more than just skills on the line. Besides, CPAs talk to each other, and they're quite aware of who's been snagged for what technical tax violation, and how to avoid the chance of an audit.

As mentioned, there are good CPAs who are reluctant to get involved with long-range tax strategies, either because they're uncomfortable with certain investment tactics, or would much rather play with an abacus all day long. This does not mean they aren't qualified to help you; it may simply mean that you are making enough money to pay for the advice of an addi-

tional advisor (never let go of a good CPA, though) who
can help you evaluate offensive moves in your tax planning. If we were to draw an analogy to football, the CPA
would be the defensive coach; your offense might well be
headed by someone who operates under the title of Personal Financial Planner.

We all know that the 1970s have been described as
the Me Decade, a period during which Americans turned
inward to discover how OK we all are after all. But
another trend began emerging in the latter part of the
decade which, although owing allegiance in part to the
psyche, had a great deal more to do with the everyday
realities of life as they pertain to economics.

Just as millions turned toward the spiritual and
psychological gurus who hold seminars and publish
books designed to optimize one's *human* potential, a
growing number of Americans have begun to seek out
more sophisticated guidance for their financial potential
in an age of diminishing economic expectations. A
political analogy would be a situation wherein Governor
Jerry Brown of California would form a partnership with
President Ronald Reagan, under the banner of Cosmic
Economics, Inc.

This trend has helped spark a boom of sorts in the
financial services industry, out of which has emerged a
growing cadre of advisors who can be loosely grouped
under the functional title of Personal Financial Planner.
They are literally coming out of the woodwork from all
sorts of interesting places, and some are having a significant impact on the way Americans are investing what's
left of their capital these days. The best of the lot, I've
discovered, have some very interesting observations to
make about tax shelters as well. Of course, as in any fast-
growing industry, there are financial planners who are
cashing in on this boom by selling services neither they,
nor their clients, fully understand, or need; but they

seem to be in a minority, and none of them will be quoted in this book.

In theory, a Personal Financial Planner is an advisor or consultant who helps you get a handle on your tax situation, maximize your after-tax return on investments, plan effectively for retirement, "noodge" your cash so it flows mostly into your pocket, set up tuition or trust funds for children and other heirs, and—most important, think some—coordinate personal financial goals with planned career moves. He or she *does not replace* a CPA, attorney, insurance agent, stockbroker, or trust officer, however. Rather, a financial planner works in concert with these other specialists to develop and implement a comprehensive plan tailored to your financial situation, expectations, and reality.

They are an odd lot of characters. They can be stockbrokers or insurance agents or CPAs or attorneys—or B School grads or security analysts. They can be a combination of any, or all, of the above. The good ones are usually proficient in, and perhaps licensed to perform, one or more of the above disciplines.

Increasingly, many of them are tacking several letters after their names on their business cards: CFP, which stands for Certified Financial Planner; or MSFS, which means Master of Science in Financial Services.

The CFP is not really such a big deal, for it is granted by the College for Financial Planning, a correspondence school of sorts in Denver which issues a certificate upon satisfactory completion of its courses. The MSFS, a relatively new form of "accreditation," may eventually carry more weight than the CFP, for it's a graduate school level, fully accredited program administered by The American College in Bryn Mawr, Pennsylvania, the same school which insurance agents attend to

become Chartered Life Underwriters (CLU), the highest
designation in the field. "You've really got to know what
you're doing when you enter the MSFS program," notes
John Sestina, who heads a financial planning firm bear-
ing his name in Columbus, Ohio. "It's tough, and no-
nonsense, but definitely worthwhile," he concludes.
With 150 clients earning an average of $100,000 annual-
ly, Sestina would seem to be qualified to take this course.

However, according to Fred Harris, former executive director of the International Association of
Financial Planners (IAFP, with 8,000 members the
largest organization of its kind), it's possible for anyone
to hang out a shingle with "Personal Financial Planner"
etched on it—and either do a good job, or get away with
it without becoming certified, accredited, or degreed.

This is not to say that the financial planning business is flooded with people who can talk a good line and
then use mirrors to come up with clear plans of action to
untangle their clients' often complex financial problems.
Rather, it implies that there are so many potential
clients who earn more than $25,000 per year who could
use these services that the opportunity to make a good
living as a financial planner has induced a great many
people to hang out that shingle. Many of these people
soon discover, however, that as John Sestina puts it, "insurance isn't always the best answer for financial security," reflecting the fact that in the early part of the 1970s,
most planners came from the ranks of insurance sales.

True, a good financial planner will help you with all
the proper insurance problems—where it all starts for
most people—but he or she will also get involved in asset
protection and accumulation, pension planning, tax
sheltering, portfolio diversification and management,
and family/estate planning. This calls for knowledge, certainly, but increasingly it seems to demand an under-
standing of the way the entire international financial

world works at large, insight into a client's personal life goals, and an ability to merge these two factors into a comprehensive plan of action which brings peaceful sleep and balanced ledgers. The good ones could each probably write a book called *The Narcissistic Investor.*

Out of this situation has recently emerged a certain breed of cat who defies stereotypical description, the kind of planner who wants to know what goes on inside his or her clients' heads. John Sestina, for example, is an ex-seminarian and English school teacher. James D. Schwartz, who heads his own firm in Denver, is an MBA with a specialty in securities analysis and Management-by-Objectives programs on a corporate level. Georgette Houghton, of The Costello Group, New York City, formerly worked in advertising sales. Terry Gill, president of Professionals' Financial Group, Ft. Worth, is a West Point graduate formerly involved in the import-export trade. I've recently met a broker from Merrill Lynch *ad nauseam* who is studying to become a financial planner, yet his background is in veterinary science and he used to train racehorses for a living. All of these people have a fascination with numbers, new-style economics, and what makes people tick. It's not surprising, then, that they're heavily involved with advising clients on tax shelters, perhaps the most emotional investment a person can make.

One of the more critical functions performed by financial planners is tax shelter evaluation. Since they serve a diversified clientele of both the very flush and the fast-track devotees, financial planners are privy to all sorts of "creative" deals which are designed for the most part to separate their clients' money from their pockets. Because of the various ways a financial planner can be compensated, however (fee, commission, or fee-plus-commission), evaluating the ability of these planners to be both sophisticated and objective is a tricky process.

Generally speaking, those financial planners who work on a fee-only basis receive a set monthly sum for their advice; you use your own stockbroker or insurance agent to execute their recommendations. In the case of a tax shelter deal, most fee-only planners refuse to take a commission from the promoter involved as well, preferring, if it's a good-looking proposition, to take a piece of the action themselves—usually for less than the limited partners pay.

It is important to recognize the difference between this *modus operandi* and that of a financial planner whose major source of income comes from the commissions received on the financial products he or she suggests you buy. This is not only a financial, but also a philosophical, difference compared to fee-only planners. There are valid arguments on both sides, of course, which is what makes the world go 'round.

Jim Schwartz, for example, jumps up and down and pitches his voice an octave higher when discussing the subject. "You just can't be objective about your recommendations if you're compensated by commission," he snorts. "Is it in your interests, or mine, if I'm compensated by someone who wants to sell you something? Who am I representing in that case? You can't have it both ways. If I take a commission, it's a conflict of interest."

Georgette Houghton arches an eyebrow at Schwartz's line of reasoning, defending compensation by commission as a generally accepted way of doing business in the financial services industry. Ms. Houghton derives most of her income from modest consulting fees, but does accept commissions when her clients follow her recommendations and use her to execute the purchases. "I'm not about to compromise my clients' financial status by selling them something they don't need," she scoffs. "If I made my money just 'churning product' to my clients, I wouldn't be in business very long."

Planners who exist by commission compensation alone, however, understandably need many clients in order to generate their own living. Most of them operate in specific areas of the country—particularly the Sunbelt —where, as one Baton Rouge planner told me, "fees are just not understood, or trusted, readily."

Needless to say, the controversy over this question has split the personal financial planning industry to a point where fee-only planners have formed their own group, SIFA, the Society of Independent Financial Advisors. This is a small, select group of planners (ironically, mostly from the Sunbelt), who can recommend a member to you if you write them c/o John Sestina, 3726 "J" Olentangy River Road, Columbus, Ohio 43214. The aforementioned International Association of Financial Planners (IAFP) is comprised of members who, for the most part, exist on commission or fee-plus-commission, and includes members of SIFA. The IAFP will refer you to a local chapter if you write them at 2150 Park Lake Drive N.E., Atlanta, Georgia 30345.

Consequently, most tax shelter opportunities suggested by fee-only planners are small, "private" deals offering no commissions in the first place, as opposed to those mass-marketed "public" deals which are packaged and sold off-the-shelf under the sponsorship of Wall Street firms, much in the same manner as new issues of stocks or bonds. (The differences between public and private tax shelters will be explained in Chapter Six.)

In any case, whether you opt for a fee-only or fee-plus-commission or commission-only planner, you ought to be able to get a good deal of free advice before choosing one by using the same essential interviewing process outlined for selecting a good CPA. The planner, however, is likely to get far more detailed with you during your preliminary meetings, putting you through not only a financial grilling, but also, if you get one of the new breed of cats, a head trip.

There is a mind-boggling array of strategies a good financial planner can suggest for you to begin to get a handle on not only your tax situation, but also your total financial picture. If a good planner or CPA has a clear picture of what you're doing with your life and your money, chances are year-round tax planning can reduce your total tax bill to a less-than-angina-inducing amount.

If you're still stuck after all this, you're now ready to confront the wonderful world of tax shelters *per se*. Fetch some pretzels or carrot sticks, a dose of valium or a strong drink, perhaps a little Maui Wowie, settle back and try not to get *too* excited as we move along.

3.

"Howdy, Pardner.
Have I Got A
Deal For You."

Get this through your head right from the start: A tax shelter is an *investment*, a security which has as its kin such other goodies as stocks, bonds, mutual funds, money-market funds, options, commodities, or bank certificates-of-deposit. As such, your primary purpose in making an investment in a tax shelter should be to make a profit on your money.

So much for fantasy.

As with any investment, tax shelters have their risks and their rewards. Unfortunately, too many people who dream up these deals, too many people who sell them, and too many people who buy them, think that both the risks and the rewards should come at the beginning of the investment cycle, when one plunks one's money down. This is something I've never been able to figure out logically, since I always thought you make a profit when you sell something you made, or previously bought, to someone else. Tax shelters, however, are different.

What you get at the beginning of a tax shelter is a loss. Hopefully, as big a loss as the amount you've put up. Ideally, a *bigger* loss than what you've invested in cash. Why? Because the peculiar risk you take in tax shelters is supposed to be so great that there's very little chance you will be successful in getting your money back, let alone embellishing it with a profit.

The risk is one which no sane capitalist would take without the chance for substantial reward. The reward in a tax shelter is the right to deduct your risk capital (or loss) from your taxable income during the year you make the investment—and if you're farsighted, in subsequent years as well.

It's all rather analagous to starting your own business. When you do that, you're allowed to deduct the costs of doing business against whatever income the business generates. If you purchase equipment to help run the business, you get certain tax breaks in the form of credits and depreciation to offset the planned obsolescence of that equipment. The same basic theories apply to tax shelter investments, except that, in most cases, more than one person is putting up the risk capital, and each person shares in the "rewards" of the write-offs.

That's all a tax shelter is: An investment in a new business venture. Indeed, the venture capitalists of the 1970s were primarily investors in tax shelters, since the climate of the stock market—and the high capital gains tax rates brought about by the Tax Reform Act of 1969 —effectively held down enthusiasm for investing in new businesses by purchasing stock. And although both stockholders and investors in tax shelters put up risk capital to own a piece of the business, the up-front

negative rewards which accrue to tax shelter investors
come about because of a peculiar quirk in the tax and
business laws which make clear delineations between the
rights of shareholders in a corporation and the rights of
those tax shelter participants, who are usually known as
partners.

That's what you become when you invest in a tax
shelter: a partner, more specifically a *limited* partner,
one who joins other limited fellows in trusting the
management of the venture to a General Partner.

Partnerships are not taxed in the same way as corporations. Whatever a partnership spends or makes in a
given fiscal period is allowed to "flow through" to each
partner as a *personal* loss or profit, respectively. This al-
location is allowed only to the extent that each partner's
share of losses or profits is defined in advance in a Partnership Agreement, which accompanies the Prospectus
or Private Placement Memorandum.

Thus, if you joined five other limited partners in putting a total of $50,000 into a business in 1982, and the
business makes no money, or generates no income, during that year, you would be allowed to deduct your portion of those "losses" on your 1982 tax return. If you put
that same amount of money into the *stock* of a new
business, you'd just have to sit tight until such time as
the company either makes a profit (raising the value of
your share) or goes out of business (giving you a disappointing, but deductible, loss).

As you can see, sometimes it pays to lose in the
capitalist system as it has evolved in 20th-century
America.

Thus, the most common form of investment you will
encounter in tax shelters is the limited partnership.
Don't be confused, however, if a limited partnership is

also referred to as a "syndicate." This is a word which means different things to different people, but according to my Random House Dictionary, a syndicate is "a group of individuals or organizations combined or making a joint effort to undertake some specific duty or carry out specific transactions or negotiations." While I would be the first to conclude that some tax shelter limited partnerships definitely look as though they were dreamed up by members of the syndicate known as organized crime, you really shouldn't be taken aback when the word "syndicate" comes up in conversation about these investments. It's just a bit of Wall Street colloquialism you'll have to get used to, similar to another word which is bandied about when discussing tax shelters: promoter.

A promoter organizes, markets (or, promotes), and manages a tax shelter investment. In every case, the promoter is *de facto* the General Partner, the *capo di tutti capi* of the limited partnership vehicle. It's the General Partner's business you're helping to finance when you become a limited partner, something for which the promoter should be terribly grateful. In a manner of speaking, the promoter expresses gratefulness by granting certain tax advantages to the limited partners. But like all good syndicators (another euphemism for General Partner), the promoter knows that he's making you an offer you can't refuse, so he remains in control of the situation throughout.

To wit: The laws governing limited partnerships give all management control and full discretionary powers to the General Partner, who, theoretically, is quite experienced in operating the business he's organizing. By extension, the limited partners are understood to have very little knowledge of the business in question, and are, therefore, neither expected—nor, by law, allowed—to participate in the operation of the business.

This is quite different from the relationship between shareholders and the management of a corporation. If the shareholders don't like what management is doing, they can band together to throw the bums out. Not so in most limited partnerships. The General Partner is king, chancellor of the exchequer, and lord high executioner; while the limited partners are the peasants of the realm. (A limited partner is even small-fry grammatically; note that General Partner is capitalized, while limited partner is not.)

Shareholders pay dearly for their right to throw the management out by not being allowed to take "flow-through" losses and profits (except in the case of Subchapter S corporations, which have fewer than 25 shareholders; but let's not confuse the issue). Correspondingly, limited partners pay dearly for their rights to claim losses (and, ho-ho, profits) by having to live with the same management for the life of the investment. The General Partner, which is nearly always a corporation, is extremely difficult, therefore, to usurp . . . and that includes suing for malfeasance or plundering of the assets of the peasants.

While there have been cases where limited partners organized to sue and remove a General Partner who was so grossly incompetent that even Cardinal Richelieu would have had compassion, understand that it's a costly, frustrating, and time-consuming process which can have dire consequences for the limited partners. Why? Well, say a group of limited partners got together and sued the General Partner for fraud, and eventually some judge somewhere concluded that this was indeed the case. What might happen next is that the IRS could step in to investigate whether the entire deal's a sham. The limited partners would then be subject to pay the very taxes they tried to avoid in the first place if the IRS so concludes. Like I said, a limited partner is a peasant, and peasants don't write the laws.

Another serious investment disadvantage of a limited partnership is that it is *illiquid* in the extreme. This means that you cannot readily sell your partnership interest to anyone—and most especially not on an open market—as you can with stocks and bonds. Some limited partnership agreements allow the sale of interests back to the General Partner at some future date, but generally speaking, you are stuck with your investment for the term of the activities covered under the prospectus or partnership agreement. This can range from one to 12 years—or forever—depending on the industry you invest in, and the way the deal is structured.

Thus, if you've invested $5,000 (usually the minimum) in a limited partnership in 1982, and you're in a marginal tax bracket, you may find that by 1984 you need $5,000 cash for an emergency. Since in those brackets you're generating a heck of a lot of tax, but not too much cash, you may be out of luck if you're in a limited partnership. If you'd put that money into stocks or bonds, you could call up your broker and sell, or put the securities up as collateral for a loan. However, you cannot call up anyone in an emergency to bail you out of a limited partnership very easily—certainly not your broker, who probably sold you the deal and has long since spent the commission. And no bank to which I've talked will accept your limited partnership interest as collateral for a loan. "Damn things are so risky, you know," said one officer of Citibank in New York.

Are you beginning to understand why tax shelters, however tempting they might be to someone who's being gorged at the 40% to 44% rates, are very, very risky investments and should only be considered as an absolute last resort by people of insufficient liquidity, no matter what tax bracket?

4.

"Numbers! Numbers! Who's Got The Numbers?"

One of the follies you're likely to run up against in today's wonderful world of tax shelters is the numbers racket. Any promoter can make it very attractive for a taxpayer in the 40% to 44% tax brackets to start dreaming thoughts of reduced tax bills, or no tax bill at all, by pulling out a calculator and pressing a few buttons. Ah, watch the numbers dance, discoing onto your tax return in curls, dips, and loopholes which will send more shivers up your spine than a heavy dose of a controlled substance taken orally or nasally.

Look out for numbers. They don't quite work out the way you want them to when you're gambling—which is what you're basically doing with a tax shelter investment. How many times have you gone to the racetrack and put a couple of bucks on the Daily Double which you figure has to pay a couple of hundred dollars because the two horses you coupled are listed at odds of 15 to 1 and 20 to 1? And how many times has that Daily Double come in and paid around $120 or so—thus upsetting your odds and your hopes and dreams? Tax shelters work the same way when it comes to numbers, especially for those who are not being hit at a rate of 49% and above.

The object of the money you put into a tax shelter is to cut your taxes by reducing your taxable income (or, Adjusted Gross Income), possibly move you into a lower tax bracket, and give you a decent shot at hitting the Daily Double by making a profit. While any reduction of taxable income might be welcomed these days, what you're really looking for in a tax shelter is to break even on the deal at the beginning by cutting Uncle Sam out of his share of whatever amount you invest—say, half. That means that for every dollar you put into a tax shelter, you want to get as much of that buck back in the form of a reduced tax bill. That can only work out profitably at the 49%-and-above tax brackets—and remember, that's 49% *after* you've done everything else possible to reduce your tax load with the help of a tax attorney, CPA, or financial planner.

The numbers, they don't lie. Let's go with a situation of a taxpayer who's in the 50% bracket. It's easier to explain tax shelter theory in nice round numbers, even though on your return things will undoubtedly look different. Later on, we'll use numbers which might more closely touch home.

Assume that after all deductions our married taxpayer (whose only income is wages) is left with taxable income of $100,000. On that amount, he would owe 50% on all taxable income over $60,000, or—ouch—$37,499 to Uncle Sam. Here's what a $10,000 investment in a 100% deductible tax shelter (assuming no tax preference items) would produce on the calculator:

	Without Shelter	With Shelter
Taxable income	$100,000	$100,000
Tax shelter (loss)	-0-	(10,000)
Taxable income	100,000	$ 90,000
Tax due	37,499	32,499
Tax savings	-0-	$ 5,000

Voilà! For every dollar invested, 50 cents is saved in taxes. From an investment point of view, the after-tax cost to the investor of the tax shelter was $5,000, which means that if the business he invested in returns $5,001, there's a profit. Charming, no?

Now, look at what happens if he invests $30,000 in a 100% deductible tax shelter:

	Without Shelter	With Shelter
Taxable income	$100,000	$100,000
Tax shelter (loss)	-0-	(30,000)
Taxable income	$100,000	$ 70,000
Tax due	37,499	22,605
Tax savings	-0-	$ 14,894

Get the picture? He's actually only put about $15,000 in hard dollars into the deal; the other $15,000 would have gone to Uncle Sam anyway.

Now, let's get a little creative with a more likely situation. A married couple filing jointly earns $80,000 per year; he's an executive with a $50,000 salary, she's a teacher earning $30,000. They have no children, few medical expenses, and the bulk of their deductions come from the mortgage they pay on their $80,000 condo. For argument's sake, let's say their joint taxable income (after all common deductions) is $60,000. At that level, they would owe 49% of the next $25,600 to Uncle Sam; and if they live in a state with an income tax, would be paying more than 50% of additional income over $60,000 in the form of taxes. But let's put them in Franconia, New Hampshire, where there is no state income tax. Here's what a $20,000 tax shelter investment would be worth to them, if every penny was deductible.

	Without Shelter	With Shelter
Taxable income	$60,000	$60,000
Tax shelter (loss)	-0-	(20,000)
Taxable income	$60,000	$40,000
Tax due	17,705	9,195
Tax savings	-0-	$ 8,510

Take another sip of your drink. What has happened here is that the tax has been reduced by 48% because the $20,000 investment has moved this couple *down* the tax bracket ladder to the 44% rung.

See how excited people can get about tax shelters?

But don't go running out to the CPA yet, especially if you're in a marginal tax bracket to begin with. Let's say that same couple is in the 33% tax bracket, with taxable income of $30,000 (they have lots of children, medical expenses, and a dog who's given birth to triplets, which—creatures as they are—the couple adopted as their own). At that level, they're not working with a heck of a lot of cash (have you noted the price of dog food lately?), so let's assume they're willing to put $5,000 into a 100% deductible tax shelter. Here's the way the numbers work out:

	Without Shelter	With Shelter
Taxable income	$30,000	$30,000
Tax shelter (loss)	-0-	(5,000)
Taxable income	$30,000	$25,000
Tax due	5,607	4,153
Tax savings	-0-	$ 1,454

That $1,454 may look like a goodly sum, but it represents only a 26% tax reduction from the $5,607 owed, a less-than-even split with Uncle Sam. This investment would have to return $3,546 for the couple to make a profit, and those odds are simply not worth the $5,000 risk to people with poor liquidity to begin with—unless they have a net worth exclusive of home and furnishings of more than $200,000. Then, *maybe,* they might want to take a chance.

These numbers still might look impressive to you, but remember that tax shelters in the 1980s are different from the deals which were peddled in the 1970s in several important respects. In the first place, finding a 100% deductible tax shelter is very tough these days—so even in the 49% bracket, the likelihood of achieving a substantial tax savings *without assuming additional risks* is very remote. In most deals (other than equipment leasing, real estate, and exotica), the best you can hope for is a 90% write-off, which means that our executive/teacher couple would probably not wind up with such a wonderful situation after all, since only $18,000 of their $20,000 would be deductible, thus throwing their mad dreams for a bit of a tumble. And a 90% write-off for someone in the 33% to 44% tax brackets reduces the advantages of a tax shelter even more dramatically. Never mind the numbers; trust me.

I know what you're going to say: *Anything* I can save is a bonus. Yes, and they still serve free sandwiches and hard-boiled eggs at lunch down at McSorley's. But they've tripled the price of beer.

5.

Only Turkeys Stick
Their Necks Out
At Thanksgiving

People who do not plan their tax lives carefully are prone to do things at the last minute. That means that when November rolls around, and the first thoughts of April 15th start creeping into their dreams, these people start scrambling for opportunities to cut their taxes. This is why the tax shelter season has traditionally fallen between Labor Day and Thanksgiving, when all the investment turkeys come home to roost.

If you've planned properly, you will have looked at the best tax shelters available in the beginning of the year, and will have made your decision as to which industry and which deal you want to go with by August at the latest. During that time, you will have had an opportunity to digest the consequences of the *real* charm in some tax shelters, a thing called "leverage." Like all charming things, the leverage factor in tax shelters lures you with wonderful promises and sexy window dressing. When you wake up, however, you may discover that like the snakes of India, or a hickey on the neck, charming things leave tracks. Tax shelters which are promoted at the end of the year are very big on leverage; those peddled earlier feature this financial ploy as well, but at least you have time during the winter and spring months to weigh one deal's leverage against the other, risk-wise.

Leverage is the act of borrowing money to buy what you want with as little cash as possible, yet still achieving certain goals. When you put a down payment on a house, you are leveraging your purchasing power, and boosting your deductions when you take out a mortgage. Tax shelters which operate on the leverage factor work on the same theory. The reality, however, can be a bird of a different feather.

Your cash investment in a tax shelter ($5,000 and up) is used as a down payment by the General Partner, the equity in the business, so to speak. The General Partner then goes out and borrows additional capital to finance the business activities of the limited partnership, from two to ten times the amount of cash invested by all limited partners. This capital can be genuine cash from a lending institution, or simply a promissory note the limited partners sign to a third party.

Sometimes, wonder of wonders, the third party actually puts up the cash; many times, however, the note is just that—a promise by the limited partners to pay a portion of their share of the venture's revenues, if any, to retire the debt. Thus, money may or may not change hands during the leverage process in a tax shelter. This is quite different than what happens when you buy a house and certified checks fly all over the place at closing.

If cash is put up, the limited partners have a problem which is covered by the words "at risk." If no money is exchanged, the problem which arises has to do with something called "fair market value." "At risk" and "fair market value" are the venomous sides of the charms of leverage.

To understand the whole story, let's begin with a look at leverage, and how it boosts tax shelter for an individual with taxable income of $100,000. Say this investor puts $10,000 cash into a limited partnership with a 300% write-off. This means that the General Partner will borrow $20,000 on behalf of the investor to boost the write-off to 3-1, or a $30,000 deduction. Here's the bottom line:

	Without Leverage	With Leverage
Taxable income	$100,000	$100,000
Tax shelter (loss)	(10,000)	(30,000)
Taxable income	90,000	70,000
Tax	$ 32,499	$ 22,605

Neat, no? Well, if you think that's terrific, can you imagine what would happen in a situation wherein our executive/teacher family with taxable income of $60,000 goes into a year-end tax shelter with a 6-to-1 write-off on a $10,000 investment? Right. They wind up with a total taxable income of *zero*. Bingo! A refund!

Zap! An audit!

Outrageous? Not if you know how desperate some people are to cheat Uncle Sam, and how easy some promoters make it appear that it can be done. Unfortunately, the IRS computers are programmed to burp when a return comes in with numbers like that, as we'll see later on in this chapter. Aside from the fact that a negative taxable income looks kind of funny, the IRS will want to know how much of the leverage is "at risk," and whether the total deduction taken represents the "fair market value" of the business activity involved in the shelter.

Take the question of "at risk." When you borrow money, whether from a bank, your Aunt Matilda, or a local loan shark, you are definitely at some risk to pay it back. The bank will repossess, your Aunt Matilda may cut you out of her will, and the loan shark may cut off one of your appendages if you welsh. Congress and the IRS feel the same about tax shelters.

As a result of the Tax Reform Act of 1976 and the Revenue Act of 1978, if you leverage any tax-sheltered investment and take a deduction based on that borrowed money, you must be "at risk" to pay off that loan legally —or you will find upon audit that your deductions will be disallowed. This is true of every tax shelter except real estate—an American sacred cow with both a rich lobby and built-in sympathy from every Congressperson who owns property and is not about to cut his or her own throat.

Some promoters will tell you that if you sign a note which technically puts you "at risk," you have no real worry because the noteholder has no intention of putting the arm on you. Ask yourself the following question: If you don't have to pay off the loan and the deal goes down the tubes, what happens when the IRS finds out the limited partnership is in Bust City? They'll want to know why the noteholder did not protect itself by calling in the loans which were allegedly "at risk." There are only two possible answers the noteholder can give with a straight face:

1. "We didn't actually advance the cash," in which case the IRS is likely to declare the whole deal a sham.

2. "We're nice people, and didn't feel like pressing the poor limited partners to the wall," in which case you were not truly on the hook to begin with. Tsk, tsk.

What might happen next is referred to as "recapture," which means basically what it sounds like it does —bad news for the limited partners.

Thus, if you go into a leveraged deal outside of real estate, you are taking an additional high risk because you must be on-the-hook —*at risk*— for the full amount of your cash and leverage in order to deduct your losses.

Then you have the problem of "fair market value," which has nothing to do with the intentions of Congress, but everything to do with the rights and powers of America's shadow government, the Internal Revenue Service.

In order to boost the deductions of limited partnerships and make their deals more attractive to desperate investors (especially at year-end), some promoters actually inflate the value of the underlying commodity of a tax shelter beyond what it would bring on the open market. They do this with leverage.

These abuses usually occur in industries which are loosely lumped by tax shelter afficionados into the category of "esoterica" or "exotica"—publishing, lithography, entertainment, mining. But they can also be found in real estate, farming, and equipment leasing. You'd be surprised at how many reasonably intelligent people stumble over the "fair market value" bugaboos of tax shelters.

A stockbroker once phoned me to chat about a tax shelter in which he was thinking of sinking $10,000 cash. Although I cautioned him at the outset that as a journalist I could offer no advice, I was willing to listen to his tale; if nothing else, it might make for interesting copy some day. See if you don't agree.

"I've got this problem," he began. "I left one firm in May with a settlement of $25,000. Now it's November, and I think I've made enough at my new firm to throw me into the 50% tax bracket. Trouble is, no taxes were withheld from that $25,000, and my accountant tells me I'll probably owe $12,500 in tax in April, on top of what I'll owe from this job."

"You seem to be in a pickle," I replied. "I hope you saved some of that $25,000."

"Oh, that's long gone," he moaned. "Inflation, you know."

"So, you're saying you don't have the money to pay the tax?"

"No. Well, yeah. I don't have the money. But I won't pay the tax."

"What do you propose to do?" I was beginning to be intrigued.

"I'm gonna put ten grand in a record deal with a 6-to-1 write-off, and get a refund on the whole kaboodle."

There was what you call a pregnant pause on the line. Understand that just a month before, the IRS had effectively put the kibosh on record tax shelters—known as "master recordings" in the trade—especially ones with outlandish leverage.

Briefly, an investor who goes into a record deal pays for the rights to a master recording of an album, which is a depreciable asset on which one can also take a 10% investment tax credit. He or she also pays advance royalties to the recording artists involved out of the leverage. The investor is repaid from the sales—if any—of the copies of the album made from the master recording. The loan is also paid off from the receipts. In this case, a $50,000 note provided the 6-to-1 write-off. Thus, if this stockbroker—let's call him Fred—put $10,000 into a 6-to-1 record deal, a combination of losses and tax benefits resulting from the investment tax credit amounting to $60,000 would flow through to his personal tax return.

At the time, the IRS had issued rulings on master lithograph programs which were structured similarly to master recordings, attacking both the "at risk" and "fair market value" aspects of these deals. Without getting into the details (which will be explained in a later chapter on these deals), it was quite obvious to me that Fred was playing with fire here.

"Er, Fred," I continued, rubbing my fingers across my forehead, "have you heard what the IRS said last month about these kinds of deals?"

"Ah, that's just a scare tactic. I went into a deal with this same outfit last year and got 7½-to-1 as a write-off. This year, they lowered the write-off so we won't look too conspicuous." He was definitely in Confidence City.

"So, why are you calling me?"

"I wanna know if you think it's a good deal."

"How the hell should I know? What happened last year? How many records did you sell?"

"Oh, I don't know. I just mailed my check off with the partnership papers to a post office box in the Bahamas . . . ."

"Whaaaaaaaat?"

"Yeah. But I didn't get nailed. Got all the proper tax forms back and everything."

"Did you ever meet these promoters? Did you ever get a copy of the record for your files at least?"

"Nah. Just sent the check."

By now, I was mildly apoplectic. After all, Fred, as a stockbroker, could be giving this advice to his clients. "Who cut the record, Fred? Did you ever see it in the stores?"

"Oh, it was some punk-rock group called Razor," he laughed. "We had this joke around the office last year, 'The Razor is cutting our record.' They probably broke up anyway after they made the album. You know these crazy kids. But," he chortled, "I got my deductions."

What was bothering me now—aside from the obvious risks Fred was running with the IRS computer— was where he got the $10,000 to invest if he was so broke he couldn't afford to pay the tax he was trying to avoid.

"I borrowed it from the bank," he chirped.

You can imagine the expletives he hurled over the phone lines when I asked my last question. "Listen, Fred, can you stand an audit?"

Not only could he not stand an audit, he couldn't run the risk of being back-audited, either, which is what usually happens when the IRS uncovers what it thinks is a pattern of tax evasion.

"Look, Fred, why didn't you just ask your former boss to withhold the tax in the first place?"

"Waddaya crazy? All that paperwork? Besides, like I said, I needed the money, and I won't pay the tax."

I casually informed Fred that if he was really serious about avoiding taxes, he should join the Underground Economy, get out from behind his stockbroker's desk and start dealing high-grade marijuana to other stockbrokers at the corner of Wall Street and Broad. In that case, he wouldn't be caught in the IRS's computer, and he could always plea-bargain.

"Hey, what kind of guy you think I am? I'm just an average middle-class slob trying to make a buck!"

Yes, Fred, me too. But a razor can definitely be a double-edged sword, a fact which I understand through the grapevine Fred has since discovered in a confrontation with the IRS.

Eric Sevareid, the media pundit, once gave the following advice to journalists and editors: "Never underestimate the intelligence of your readers. Never overestimate their need for information." When it comes to tax shelters, that phrase can be twisted a bit to read: "Never underestimate the risks you face on every front. Never overestimate the fair market value of your investment."

Part Two

Three On A Match:
Investor, Promoter,
Taxman

6.

Everybody
Wants To Be
Cosimo de' Medici

In his marvelously austere and objective trilogy, *The Age of the Medici*, the late Italian film director Roberto Rossellini included a scene which could have come right out of the fantasies of a 20th-century anarchist. The setting is 15th-century Florence, dominated by the powerful banking family headed by Cosimo de' Medici. The scene in question takes place in the tax collector's office, where the Florentines have been summoned to cough up taxes in order to finance a war which has been "scheduled" against a neighboring city-state.

First to be assessed is a local peasant, whose total assets and income for the year total 40 gold florins. In a straightforward manner, the tax collector tells the peasant that the tax due is eight florins, or 20% of his assets and income. The peasant mutters and mumbles, sputtering off-camera with expletives designed to reach the ears of the next person in line, the accountant for the Medici clan.

There is some deference on the part of the tax collector to the Medici accountant. The taxman proceeds to enumerate the Medici holdings and income, while the accountant follows along with his own ledger. In time, the Medici's net worth is determined to be 120,000 florins—which one would think would result in a rather hefty war tax for the Republic. Here, however, the Medici accountant takes over, carefully listing all the deductions and exemptions to which the household is entitled, including those taken for servants, 22 members of the extended family, losses on certain business transactions, investment credits, and donations to the commonweal, etc. With the supplicating tax collector nodding appreciably, the accountant for the Medici manages to reduce the tax owed on a base of 120,000 florins to 560 florins, a less than one-half of one percent assessment.

It is not inconceivable that the father of the Renaissance, Cosimo de' Medici, may also have planted a few seeds in the garden of tax shelters.

I bring up this vignette to illustrate the point that in today's wonderful world of high taxes, fast living, bountiful and inflated dollars, social pressures, and Betamax dining schedules, more than a few people have developed a Medici complex. Building upon assets and income from their everyday jobs, these people have tried to accumulate impressive estates by investing in securities and deals which appreciate, and throw off both cash flow and prestigious cocktail party chatter at the same time. Some discover that, through ingenious massaging of a few loopholes in the Tax Code, they can actually increase their net worth and decrease their tax exposure substantially by approaching life as if they were to the manner born, i.e., with a degree of patience and an eye for the right opportunity combined with a marvelous sense of timing. Far more, however, try to move too quickly into the robes of a Medici, making commoners' mistakes along the way which tend to keep them forever casting about as well-paid, but indentured, peasants.

It is a combination of both the mundane and exciting industries that make up the world of tax shelters which leads to a Medici complex. The most popular of these industries have a certain amount of glamour and folklore attached to them—glamour in the form of social acceptability, folklore in the respect that vast fortunes have been built in the past by people who exploited these industries. One would have to look very hard to find a more diverse and incongruous group of businesses to invest in than those which are most often thought of when "tax shelter" is mentioned: oil and gas drilling, real estate, mining for coal, diamonds or gold, equipment leasing, farming, livestock breeding, horseracing, publishing, movies, artwork and lithography, charitable giving—this is the portfolio of an educated, sophisticated, cunning and *respected* individual.

In truth, who wouldn't mind having a few wells pumping away, an office building or two located in the heart of the high-rent district, a place in the country where one breeds Black Angus and milks Guernseys, a piece of a magazine with a climbing circulation, a couple of potential Derby winners in the barn, and a storehouse full of rapidly appreciating lithographs waiting to be scooped up by art nouveau collectors from Portland to Paducah? Dreams are the stuff of tax shelters. But how many times have you been rolling along in a dream when suddenly things go wrong and you wake up in a cold sweat? Tax shelters may have their roots in dreams, but then again, so do nightmares.

Bad dreams and bad deals can be avoided, however. One should not eat a world-record banana split immediately before retiring if one expects to get through the night relatively intact. In the same way, one would be foolish to contemplate a tax shelter in which the activities of the venture are such that they give one a case of *agita* every day. Tax shelters are businesses where everything has to go right, but something usually goes wrong along the way. To the degree that an investor understands what *can* go wrong, and what shouldn't happen at all, is a clear function of education. Dealing with things which *go* wrong, and preventing things which shouldn't happen, is a clear function of management.

An investor in a tax shelter should not be expected to manage the way the business goes; but one should certainly understand how the business works before plunking down one's money. Above everything else, Cosimo de' Medici was an educated man, one who made decisions only after assembling all the facts at his disposal, after satisfying his curiosity. An investor who has delusions of grandeur, or simply hopes of not being pummeled financially, should possess the curiosity and intuition which is needed to become educated about the prospects of a tax shelter's success.

The best way to satisfy one's curiosity about tax shelters is to study the various industries you might be interested in from several points of view:

(1) *What are the chances of economic success in the particular industries?* While promoters and brokers will sometimes exaggerate the chances of success in drilling an oil well in Chicago or building an office tower near Mt. St. Helens, most ventures in any tax shelter favored industry *are* considerably less far-fetched but also may be as decidedly risky. The vast majority of wells drilled (six out of seven) are dry; for every Olympic Tower on Fifth Avenue in New York, there's an Omni Complex trying to steer away from bankruptcy in Atlanta; for every Spectacular Bid there are three turkeys in the barn who can't pay their own feed bills.

You can do some pretty decent research on any of the industries which interest you, but this is sometimes difficult to begin, especially for people busy developing Medici complexes. You can start, of course, by reading the rest of this book, which should give you some kind of insight into what goes on in these businesses.

Aside from this self-effacing advice, visits to your local library to research articles which have recently appeared on tax shelters in general, or a particular industry's economic outlook are an oft-overlooked source of insightful information. Most large cities have periodical sections in their main branches, and you'd be surprised at what a day spent cross-referencing articles listed in the *Reader's Guide to Periodic Literature* can do for one's education. You may, for example, be interested in checking out the economics related to drilling an oil or gas well—the primary business activity of an oil/gas tax shelter. Well, there are bound to be articles from *The Oil & Gas Journal, Western Oil Reporter, The Oil Daily,* or even *Business Week* on the topic—or subjects touching upon the topic. The news of a business lies in the trade publications of that business—not on the business pages of the daily papers. Similarly, you might be interested in the current state of the art market as specifically related to lithographs or rare, limited edition artbooks. There, for your perusal, are thousands of words on the topic, appearing in publications ranging from *Art in America* to *The New York Times* "Weekend" section. You could read *The Blood-Horse* to get a line on Thoroughbred racing trends and statistics, and at least a dozen real estate publications to find out the latest way of making bucks in that industry.

Never underestimate the power of a library to educate, for it brings you knowledge on a one-to-one basis, without the bias of commercial exploitation to motivate it. In other words, no salesperson will call.

During the course of this rummaging, you will probably see a number of "experts" quoted in various places, particularly in articles where tax shelters are discussed. You will soon discover that for a multibillion dollar bunch of industries, the tax shelters of today have relatively few "spokesmen." This has come about for two reasons: (a) These guys have excellent public relations representatives who, coincidentally, have clients who can stand the test of time in a business saturated with failure, and who can respond to the insufferably stupid questions we journalists ask. (b) They are an easy interview and good copy in print. A loose network of good old boys in Brooks Brothers suits has developed in the tax shelter industry as a whole during the past ten years, crossing over regions, industries, and philosophies. Included are stockbrokers, promoters, CPAs, attorneys, financial planners, and investment bankers—all of whom scratch each other's backs to promote tax shelters as a whole, while boosting their favorite industries at the same time.

Despite the fact that we journalists tend to come down hard, philosophically and between-the-lines, when it comes to writing about tax shelters, what will emerge from your research is a fairly honest and accurate picture of what's usually happening in your chosen industry. Of course, you can check the reporting in articles on tax shelters against the stories which are running in any trade publications covering the industry you're interested in to make sure the tax shelter experts know what they're talking about.

(2) *What are the tax advantages indigenous to each industry, and which are likely to stand IRS scrutiny?* There are a number of newsletters which discuss tax shelters, and several seminars conducted each year in various key cities which you might be interested in attending. As far as seminars are concerned, I would be very careful about attending one which is sponsored by a brokerage firm in conjunction with a promoter to explain the details of a given industry. What you'll get is smooth

talk for a particular deal, which is quite different from attending a seminar in which several experts sit around chatting about the sorry state of world affairs. Take the sponsored seminars with a grain of salt, and if you choose to pay to attend an "independent" seminar, spend as much time as you can picking the brains of experts during coffee and meal breaks.

When it comes to newsletters, you'll find *Brennan Reports* and *The Stanger Report* to be as far as you might want to go. The former, which comes from the desk of Bill Brennan, a CPA whose background includes years of financial wizardry for coal companies, has been around a little longer, and approaches tax shelters and tax planning in a detailed, nitpicking, sometimes tongue-in-cheek manner. Brennan works out of Valley Forge, Pennsylvania, and will review particular deals—public or private—either directly or obliquely in his newsletter each issue.

Robert Stanger's entry into the tax shelter newsletter field does not review specific deals per se, but rather approaches the subject in a how-to, hands-on manner. It's breezier—and more expensive—than Brennan's, and serves the purpose of reading like an armchair advisor. Stanger is also a bit chattier than Brennan, although this is not said as a criticism of either style; it's simply a matter of approach, and each man's individuality comes through in his newsletter. Both these publications are widely read, so you might ask your stockbroker for a sample copy of each so that you can get a feel of which you want to subscribe to—if not both.

Much of the basic tax data pertaining to each kind of tax shelter will be found in later chapters of this book, but the common sense rule to follow when reviewing tax angles of given deals is: does it make sense to me, or does it seem to be a bit cute? Tax shelters which hold up to

IRS scrutiny are always those which are based on conservative interpretations of the Tax Code.

You may also wish to obtain sample copies of prospectuses of various kinds of tax shelters from your broker or CPA. These documents are usually written by attorneys who have one eye on the Securities and Exchange Commission, and another on the promoter who is paying the bill. Thus, they usually come out reading like the Bronx white pages, if that exciting. But it pays to scrounge up a few recent deals of all types to get the lay of the land, so to speak. At least you won't have a blank stare on your face when a promoter explains tax aspects to you if you actually go out shopping for a deal. Besides, you'd be surprised at the intelligent questions you can ask a promoter about taxes when you know the difference between accelerated and straight-line depreciation, intangible and completion expenses, preference items and tax credits.

If you are serious about reducing your taxes legally, you are simply going to have to understand how things *work*. Boring as it might sound, a couple of evenings spent reviewing the tax angles of various kinds of shelters is time well-spent. Brew lots of espresso to keep awake, however.

(3) *How close do I want to be to my investment?* The word "close" here is used to define both one's proximity to the main business activity, and one's subjective attitude toward the business involved. In other words, are you the type of person who can send $5,000 or $25,000 off in an envelope to some promoter clear across the country and then take your chances that the well will be drilled, the apartment house purchased and maintained, the cattle fed, the equipment delivered and working, the horse in training, or the book distributed? Or, are you the kind of person who prefers to keep an eye on your

money while it's working, as close to home as possible, and in a business which you understand and enjoy?

This is a crucial factor in choosing a tax shelter investment, especially if you're one of those people who don't sleep well to begin with. To some people, watching a well being drilled is the most exciting thing in the world; knowing that it's being drilled only a short drive from home is heaven. To others, the prospect of owning part of a luxury office building clear across the country is just as satisfying, if only because it feeds a part of the ego.

There are ways to have your investment and watch it, too, when it comes to selecting the right tax shelter industry, and the proper deal to invest in. First, you must be totally objective about your investment and personal goals. Do you want to use tax shelters merely to reduce taxes, and take as a bonus anything which comes your way in the form of return-on-investment? In this case, you may prefer to invest in "public" deals, investments which are registered with the Securities and Exchange Commission, and which are usually marketed nationwide by stockbrokers and other high-powered sales forces to any and all "qualified" comers. These deals usually seek to raise from $5 million to $100 million in cash, and tend to spread their business activities all over the country, if not all over the globe. The most common industries for publicly offered deals are oil/gas drilling, real estate, cattle feeding, equipment leasing, and the occasional "masterwork" which has become all the rage in any particular year.

A public deal has the advantage of having been "cleared" by the SEC, and the disadvantage of being big enough to make a very loud noise if it crashes. Now, let's understand something about the SEC. Just because a deal has been registered with the SEC and has come through its investigation process does not necessarily mean that it's a good deal. All it means is that the SEC has taken perhaps three to six months, and the promoter has spent at least $100,000 in legal and printing costs (which the investor will eventually pay) to get some kind of assurance that the SEC feels all the factors which could affect this security's viability—including conflicts of interest—*have been disclosed.* Nowhere in a prospectus which has been cleared by the SEC will you find any indication that the deal has been "approved." Indeed, on the front page of the prospectus, there will a boldface disclaimer to the contrary.

A public deal seeking to raise millions of dollars from hundreds or perhaps thousands of individuals must be marketed across state lines by a sales force which is associated in some way with a securities dealer. In order for this to happen, such a deal must go through the "due diligence" process of the SEC, in order to satisfy the brokerage firms which may offer the deal that everything about the business and the promoter has been disclosed in advance so that should something go wrong, the chance of major lawsuits based on nondisclosure is eliminated. In other words, a public deal is a protection device for the promoters and the marketers, not necessarily for the investors alone. And don't let anyone ever tell you anything different.

Public deals, by their very nature, often engage in activities which are far-flung, and which—to say the least—have very little human attachment to them. The organizers are the conglomerateers of tax shelters, scooping up huge buildings and gobbling up mineral leases, engaging in major equipment purchases, or feeding thousands of head of cattle. A participation in a publicly offered tax shelter deal is about as intimate as the relationship an owner of 100 shares of IBM has with the development of a new computer line from that corporation. This kind of deal may, or may not, appeal to you.

Private deals, on the other hand, would seem to offer a few personal advantages over the public type—but they are the repository of the most outrageous frauds as well. In the first place, private deals are restricted by law to less than 35 investors—and in many cases, far less than this number wind up participating.

Private placements are of two generic types: (a) the kind which is structured in advance, and then hopefully sold to as many people whose tax situations and personal psychological balance can tolerate the conditions of the deal; (b) those tailored to the needs of a handful of people with similar tax situations and similar business interests.

In most cases, the tax aspects of a private deal may be a bit more adventurous than those found in publicly offered shelters. This comes about for two reasons, one rather practical, the other a bit more cynical.

First, when a public deal is structured, the tax aspects have to be fairly conservatively drawn in order to pass through the SEC without too many questions, and to appeal to as many taxpayers as possible. Thus, public deals hit the "lowest common denominator" when it comes to tax angles. Private deals can be a bit more creative on the tax side because it's often possible to find a wider variety of tax options to include since the base market (generally made up of heavy hitters, or local peers) is far more flexible in its needs.

The other reason the tax angles of private deals are sometimes more creative is that the IRS is simply not set up properly to monitor all the private deals which are sold daily in this country. While a big, fat, fully registered prospectus for a public deal is rather inviting for the IRS to peruse, simply because it's *there*, out in public (and the IRS can always get a list of the limited partners easily), such is not the case with private deals.

It's difficult to detect a widespread pattern of creative tax avoidance among millions of tax returns where perhaps only a handful have taken deductions based on some private tax shelter transaction involving real estate, energy, farming, or any other kind of business venture. In the case of private deals, it's often the local IRS auditor who calls the shots on possible audit—and oftimes this poor person is just as confused as the rest of us when it comes to interpreting the Tax Code.

I'll give you an interesting example. A few years ago, an investor in an oil and gas drilling program advised the promoter of the bad news that he was undergoing a fearful audit. The IRS was questioning some of the deductions, the investor said. The promoter in question had a good reputation for not fooling around with less-than-equitable tax arrangements, in fact, pretty much stuck to the basic deductions allowed, like intangible drilling expenses, the heart and soul of an oil/gas shelter. The promoter assured the investor any challenge would hold up. The investor was not so sure since he'd been informed by the auditor in question that under the Tax Code, *intangible drilling expenses were not allowed to be deducted* on a personal income tax return. After a bit of incredulous—and nervous—laughter, the promoter got on the next plane and met with the auditor's supervisors, who cleared up the mess rather quickly. The auditor in this case was fairly new to the job and had not been completely trained in the nuances of tax shelters. The interesting thing is that this occurred in Florida, which has had its share of petroleum development for a number of years. It should, therefore, be a state where IRS auditors have some familiarity with the ins-and-outs of the business. But such are the vagaries of life in the bureaucracy.

Other than tailor-made tax packages, private deals have the flexibility of being conducted as close to the investor's home as possible, and in a business which the investor either likes, or understands to the point that he or she is not bored with the prospect of visiting the investment from time-to-time to ascertain what's going on.

It's my belief that if you're looking for a tax shelter in which you can invest and have some emotional attachment, you'd do best to look for a private deal as close to home as possible in a business which you like. It should be organized by people you know, personally or by reputation, people who have just as much to lose as you do because they are asking you for money to help run their business. You can get together with a few other investors (through your CPAs, attorneys, brokers, financial planners, bankers) and drill wells, purchase and lease small equipment, buy and operate a herd of dairy cows, race or breed a few horses, purchase and rent out a string of one-family homes or condos or an office building in your own town, state, or area within a few hours traveling.

Time and again, the investors I've seen who take their tax shelter investments seriously—i.e., ventures where they pay attention to the economic factors and tax advantages simultaneously, but always stress the economic—are the ones who wind up doing far more with these investments than the ordinary Joe or Jane who merely sends $5,000 off to a stockbroker to buy a unit in a public deal. The serious tax shelter investors who operate on a private basis, who do the homework necessary, who get involved in understanding the operations, economics, and tax aspects of a particular industry, are the Cosimo de' Medicis of this game—the people who can build wealth and minimize tax exposure with timely, prudent investments in tax-favored industries.

Such a process is not for the impatient soul. If you're more concerned with getting a huge tax write-off or making a killing in one particular deal, you'd be just as well advised to go into a pyramid investment scheme. You're too intense for this tax shelter stuff.

7.

A Promoter By Any Other Name Still Must Be Checked Out

Every decade breeds its own particular species of entrepreneur, and the 1970s delivered a pip in the form of the tax shelter promoter. With the onset of high inflation born of the policies of the 1960s (which risked high budget deficits in order to pay for an unpopular war), the 1970s were made even more fertile years for tax shelter promoters because of the Tax Reform Act of 1969.

This charming piece of legislation must be considered a landmark in the history of capitalism, for it nipped in the bud any thought that one could take a risk with one's hard-earned money by investing in securities or activities which could be sold after a short period of time at a much higher price. Among other things, this Act raised the tax on capital gains to 48%. Now, just who do you think is going to want to hand over almost half of his or her killing to the government? I mean, that's coming very close to punishing a person for making a tidy, or heinous, profit.

The psychological effect on people with money to *risk* (and, most especially, on their advisors) was rather profound. Combined with the nasty little mess in the back rooms of Wall Street during 1968-70, one could come up with the conclusion that Truth, Justice, and the American Way might be in for a bit of a jolt, economically, if all this business about capital gains got out of hand.

Well, it did get out of hand. Between 1969 and 1975, the amount of money funneled into new equity offerings plunged from the near billion dollar per year levels of the late 1960s to $10 million in 1975. Money fled the risk-taking market to the safety of income-producing investments or ones which offered tax advantages. A steady source of income to meet the rising tide of inflation became the subliminal watchword of the day. Aided and abetted by three recessions within a decade, this national investment strategy ran smack into the reality that the more one earned to keep up with inflation, the more one paid through the nose in taxes—thanks, in part, to that wonderful Tax Reform Act of 1969. Literally overnight the investment strategy of a nation became defensive, going against the entire psychological history of a nation which was used to taking the bull by the horns, so to speak.

It became fairly obvious that something had to be done about the situation, and so, to the rescue—as entrepreneurs have done since the founding of this insane Republic—came the tax shelter promoters with the ideal situation: a tax loss which has the chance of generating income at lower tax rates than capital gains. What a terrific way to play the game. And there were so many ways one could play that it became quite fashionable at the beginning of the decade to discuss one's tax shelter over drinks at the club. In those days, there were a whole bunch of characters crawling all over the country looking for wallets to loot, dispensing favors up and down Wall Street, massaging the tax libidos of CPAs and attorneys, mouthing the buzzwords and dropping the hints at just the right places, tantalizing hundreds of thousands of Americans with dreams of oil wells pumping away with their names on them, or building government-subsidized housing projects in Selma and collecting a share of the rent from the very people you very well knew could hardly afford to put food on the table, if they weren't on welfare already, in which case you get to collect it from the government on *both* ends of the deal.

These were the tax shelter promoters, the landmen, the brokers, the whiz kids, the charlatans—the usual number of scoundrels it takes to build an industry.

I was fortunate to have watched this industry grow from somewhat of an insider's position. In 1970, I took a job as an account executive with a growing New York public relations firm after spending 18 months as a publicist for the United Way. To go from pitching a guilt trip (so people would contribute to charity) to pitching rampant consumerism (i.e., consume! consume! consume!), was just one of the cultural shocks waiting for me. The other was the fact that my first account was a guy who was interested in pitching himself as the tax shelter expert of New York. I consulted my beads and came up with both a question and an answer to deal with this dilemma:

Q. Why would an anarchist like you want to represent some fat-cat, tax-dodging cretin whose business is sure to make you puke?

A. You've got a wife and two kids, so shut up and deal.

It's amazing what a little perspective will do for a man. My first client, as it turned out, gave me tremendous insight into both the nature of man and the nature of tax shelters, warts and all. His name was David A.

Gracer, and when I met him he was a terribly charming young successful mutual fund salesman who'd done so well in that mania of the 1960s that he'd established his own company. Somewhere along the line, some of his clients became interested in oil and gas tax shelters, which at that time were being peddled as mutual funds for the rich guy. David, who had an inquisitive and highly creative mind, educated himself with a vengeance. What he saw was a concept and deals, which were ripe for potential, but at the mercy of inept, or as he put it, "less than gracious" individuals. David was inherently the type of person who sought out the good in a subject or another person, perhaps because he was a true philosopher, or perhaps because he simply wished to be prepared for life's disappointments. In any case, David saw —good businessman that he was—a perfect opportunity to: (a) help his clients, and (b) use the clout of his clients to effect changes in an industry which would benefit his clients more than the promoters.

For back in the early 1970s, David Gracer's clients were facing a virtual stampede of tax shelter peddlers who couldn't keep the deals coming fast enough, nor the terms stringent enough, for the public to consume. With so many dollars chasing so many deals, one would have to look long and hard to find the "gracious" man among the rest of the promoters. David was not the only man around at that time to reach the same conclusion; there were thoughtful bankers, stockbrokers, oil men, real estate professionals, salespersons, accountants, and attorneys who felt pretty much along the same lines. Along with David, they began finding their way into print as the nation's media discovered business and financial news consisted of much more than what happened in the stock market the day before.

Slowly, and sometimes against great odds, these people succeeded in bringing an element of class to an industry which was always a bit down in the shoes to begin with. Unfortunately, what happened at the beginning of the 1970s may be repeating itself today: The market is growing so fast that more and more promoters are coming back into the game, bringing with them twists on an old theme, enticing people with dreams of exotic profits and mysterious tax losses—"If only you sign over ten grand to me, Toots."

My relationship with David Gracer led me into more associations with people who were part of the emerging tax shelter cabal. During the next few years, at that agency and later in my own, I represented or was approached to represent consultants, drillers, real estate companies, equipment leasing firms, cattle feeders, Thoroughbred racers, and an occasional exotic entrepreneur. I even became involved in a sports franchise which was designed as a tax shelter—as most professional teams were set up prior to the expansion glut. I had come full circle—from one who got a queasy feeling when the words tax shelter were mentioned, to one who was frantically scurrying about trying to interest people in pumping some loose change into a hockey team in middle Georgia named the Macon Whoopees. When the Whoopees failed to raise the money, and went down the tubes—or out with the ice water—on Valentine's Day, 1974, I'd had enough exposure to the tax shelter business to come to a few basic conclusions about promoters. After following the field for another half-decade, I find these observations still hold true:

All tax shelter promoters are divided into three parts.

First, there are those who originate deals to satisfy a genuine economic and social need. They are experienced businesspeople who have a serious commitment to both the industry involved and the success of their particular enterprise, despite all the risks. The people who run these tax shelters—be they in oil, real estate, whatever—are smart enough to know that if they should overcome the odds and hit a gusher, or win the Kentucky Derby, their investors would not worry too unduly about the tax treatment of such a consequence. These people, in short, do not mind trying to conquer the world. Perhaps a dozen or so come out of the woodwork each year.

The second kind of tax shelter promoters are the genuinely sincere entrepreneurs who are both so broke and obsessed with a desire to conquer their own insecurities that they must take in partners who perhaps would not normally choose to be their partners (the feelings are usually mutual) if it were not for the substantial tax benefits involved. The resulting pressures are usually too much for the entrepreneur involved; i.e., do you strive all you can for a profit, or throw in a few losses along the way to keep the investor's tax advisors happy? This kind of tax shelter usually creates schizophrenia in the entrepreneur; the investors in such ventures tend to run in packs, the kind which keep the manufacturers of Maalox and Pepto Bismol very happy. It is not surprising that many investors in such tax shelters tend to be doctors and other sympathetic individuals.

The third kind of tax shelter promoter offers a deal which is simply too good to be believed. Hence, it is the most popular form of investment one can possibly search for, quickly oversubscribed by hordes of paranoid, greedy people eager to both screw the government and make a killing down the line. It goes without saying that them that gets both screwed and killed in such deals do not include the peddlers who dream them up. These are the true "promoters" of tax shelters in the pejorative sense; usually the only thing which gets promoted in these deals is the General Partner's bank account, which graduates from the U.S. to Liechtenstein.

If there's one thing axiomatic about tax shelters it's that a good deal goes hand-in-hand with a competent promoter. "Sometimes the people behind the deal count more than the deal itself," is a line I've heard over and over again from investors, advisors, and pundits on the tax shelter trail. Thus, in sizing up the potential of a given deal, one should take the time to meet the people who've organized it—and will manage it on your behalf.

Under no circumstances should an individual with $5,000 or more to risk in a tax shelter fail to meet face-to-face with the people who will eventually wind up with the money. This is especially crucial when the promoter is headquartered in another city. There will be occasions when that promoter will visit your town—and he should make arrangements to meet you if he's interested in getting your business. If the promoter has not scheduled a visit to your town, and you're still interested in investing, visit his office yourself. First, the cost of the trip is tax-deductible—even if you do not go into the deal. Second, you'll meet this person eye-to-eye on his own turf. Third, you'll get a feeling about how he might operate his business (and use your money) by observing the way he *occupies* his turf.

Some people are comfortable knowing those who manage their money have offices in the poshest district, with the best furniture, and rugs which allow you to sink in up to your eyeballs. Others are more impressed with an understated address and more modest surroundings. The question of who's paying for the trappings is usually the dividing line between opinions on the matter. The higher the management fee charged by the promoter, the posher the surroundings tend to be in most tax shelter deals. This can be shrugged off by some people, but others will look more closely at a prospectus or private placement memorandum to determine whether past economic performance justifies such exclusive surroundings. A few hours spent in the presence of an individual who manages a business will give you a definite insight into the chances you have of coming out of a deal with your money, and wits, intact. If the promoter decides to treat you to lunch at the flashiest place in town—complete with dancing girls—that may be very impressive indeed, for the promoter. If, instead, he takes you to a private club, or invites you to a quiet place where you can hold a more serious discussion, you're likely to get much more of an insight into the way this person conducts his business, because you will have noted how he conducts himself.

It's far more important to go through this trouble if you're heading into a private deal, for fewer details of a promoter's background have to be disclosed in private placement documents. In addition, a higher ticket is usually required to get into a private deal, which makes your financial risk greater than in a nationally syndicated public deal where you might put only $5,000 as compared to $20,000 or more for a private deal. If you're heading toward a public deal, don't fail to meet the promoters either; you may not have to spend so much time with them, but an experienced businessperson can usually tell within a few minutes with another businessperson whether or not the chemistry is right to do business. If your stomach tells you there's something queasy about this promoter, look for another deal.

Here are some other common sense tidbits to keep in mind when it comes time to checking out the promoter behind a deal:

• Check out the promoter's credit. This information should be in the prospectus of a public offering, but you may have to dig deeper in a private placement. Ask for a list of credit references from industry suppliers and financial institutions, and then, just as a hedge, see if you can run an independent credit check on the promoter yourself. This will give you a better idea of his assets, credit history, and other potential "insider" information.

• Pay close attention to the qualifications of the promoter's professional staff. See if you can get some kind
of references on their competence in the field—this is
true of the people who will be managing the operations
(selecting the drilling leases, acquiring properties,
writing equipment leases), and those who are responsible
for the tax and financial aspects of the business. A good
tip-off as to how seriously your investment will be
treated by the promoter would be the people he's got in
the other officers' spots. Vice presidents who are basically marketing people might be fine, so long as there are
vice presidents from the operating side as well. If there
are too many salespeople at the top of a promoter's
masthead, consider going with a company with lousy
salespeople but vice presidents who actually do the work
of the business.

• You might ask your CPA or attorney for any insight he or she might be able to give on the promoter's
independent CPA or law firm. While professionals are
reluctant to discuss such matters with lay people, if you
know your CPA or lawyer well enough, he or she is more
than likely to drop the right hints in your direction. I
have seen interesting deals in real estate compromised
because the attorneys who structured the legal and tax
aspects had little experience in real estate law, but a
whole lot in divorce actions. Somehow, the two just don't
mix, property settlements aside. Then again, an accountant who may be thoroughly experienced in the nuances
of equipment leasing may not have the foggiest notion of
the loopholes one can plunder when it comes to farming.

• Since the promoter is the General Partner, he
should have some of his own money—and his company's
cash—in the deal. If he doesn't, part of your investment
may be appropriated to give him a position in the deal.
Should that be the case, more than 20% of your investment may be siphoned off at the front end to cover the
General Partner's expenses. That's fine for the pro-

moter, but leaves much less money working for you. It
may also mean that the promoter's finances are pretty
shaky. If that's the case, the partnership you're involved
in may not be able to weather the financial crises which
seem to crop up in this country with depressing regulari-
ty every four years or so. "It really comes down to a matter of 'I win, you win, I lose, you lose,' " notes financial
planner Jim Schwartz of Denver. "I want to see the General Partner take a risk, make commitments to the
operations of the venture. I sleep a lot better at night
knowing the promoter has a good chunk of his cash tied
up in a deal."

• Check out fee schedules to see if they're reasonable. Front-end commissions for stockbrokers should be
no higher than 8% (and even that's too high, in my opinion, for simply acting as a middleman; but that's the way
the world works). In addition, you will almost always
have to pay some kind of management fee to the promoter, most of the time off the top, some of the time
coupled to incentive clauses based on the partnership's
performance. Anything above 5% on the front end is
obscene, in a public deal involving millions of dollars; a
graduated scale of fees based on performance might be
OK, depending on the business at hand, in a private deal.

In general, there are very few guidelines one can give
about these fees, for the practices within each industry
vary so greatly. For example, in real estate, there are
loads of hidden fees which are often overlooked; the promoter could have an affiliated company collecting commissions on the sale of real estate to the partnership
usually amounting to 6% of the deal. I've seen publicly
offered deals where up to 21% of the $50 million or so
raised for the acquisition of real estate actually went out
to brokers of all kinds, mostly insiders, in the form of
fees. Some promoters will tell you such is the nature of
the business. And this might be true, relatively speaking. Certainly, in the acquisition and sale of livestock

such as cattle and horses, commissions and markups can be high. My own opinion is the more money raised, the lower the proportion that should go out in front-end fees.

• Be alert to conflicts-of-interest, perhaps the most uncomfortable sign of shenanigans. These are usually spelled out in public deals, but in private offerings, you may have to look hard and ask a lot of questions to uncover the conflicts. The business of tax shelters is rife with conflicts-of-interest; it is the nature of the beast for these things to be unavoidable at times. But they should be the kind which you, as a businessperson, would be comfortable with should they occur in your business. I'm not pushing for "situational ethics" here, but rather accepting a bit of life's reality.

Some of the conflicts you can live with include past activities of the promoter which might have a better chance of succeeding than your deal. Sometimes a fairly successful entrepreneur will branch out of his original, do-it-yourself style of business and bring in partners in order to capitalize on a successful formula. Perhaps he's drilled oil wells in the past, or built and acquired office buildings on his own, wheeling and dealing in ways which are impossible to continue with a bunch of limited partners. Now he's attempting to expand his base of wealth by going into bigger deals which require vast amounts of capital, and different business structures. He might have some really good deals of his own still pumping or depreciating away, and if the deal he puts together for you falls apart, you might feel a bit miffed that he's still doing OK by his past. Well, that's not necessarily as much of a conflict as it would be if he were still putting together private deals of his own while organizing others in which investors would participate. The question which would arise would be: Why didn't he keep both deals for himself, or offer both to the public? A conflict-of-interest in a tax shelter is one in which too many questions can be answered with a shrug of the shoulders.

• If the promoter is willing to put all the investors' funds into an escrow account and pay a competitive rate of interest on the money if the partnership is not activated, he probably has the clout to raise all the money in time to meet his legal deadline. Be careful, however, of the *spread*—the difference between the amount a promoter hopes to raise and the minimum needed to activate the partnership. If the promoter can activate a $3 million partnership with $100,000 in the bank, the deal's business clout may be compromised, and the tax objectives hurt. This is also a tip-off that the promoter may be seriously deficient in making a living any other way but in activating tax shelter ventures and living off the front-end management fees from year-to-year.

Six Red Flags Over Tax Shelters

In addition to the above advice, here are some of the most commonly overlooked bugaboos promoters try to sneak past potential investors:

(1) Tax shelters should be readily understandable, not filled with exotic mumbo jumbo. Essentially, they are boring in their technical aspects, but readily understandable when someone takes the time to explain the tax angles. If you don't understand how the tax angle works after the promoter has explained it, chances are, neither does he. What's more certain, neither will the IRS. The more complicated the angle, the bigger the potential trap.

(2) Make sure the offering statement or prospectus contains an attorney's tax opinion—and in the case of public offerings, an IRS ruling, or a solid reason why it's not there (ample prior precedence, with cases cited for your attorney to check out). In private deals, the longer

the tax opinion (and the fewer the names of the partners on the law firm's letterhead) the greater the chance that you're running into big tax trouble. A private placement with a 30-page attorney's letter, 10 pages explaining what the deal is all about, and a paragraph on the promoter, is not exactly the kind of deal I'd consider as standing a decent chance of making it through the audit procedure intact.

(3) The sexier the product (toy molds, ancient bibles, gold, diamonds, mix-and-match), the tougher the tax consequences might be, to say nothing of the investment potential. Anything cute is a red flag to the IRS computer.

(4) If a broker-dealer is not underwriting or offering the deal on a best-efforts basis, chances are it may not have passed a securities firm's tough due-diligence guidelines. The names of the underwriters of a public deal, if any, will be on the front page of the prospectus. Private placements are never underwritten, although they frequently come through the offices of stockbrokers, accounting or legal firms, and bank trust departments. This does not make such a private deal a sure bet, however; it may simply be a favor being exchanged. The economic merits of the deal must still pass muster, even if you get wind of it from your Uncle Charley, the attorney.

(5) If the deal originates in a town not known as a financial center, or one which is not historically linked to the business at hand, double-check the reasons a promoter has chosen to locate there. Many tax shelters seem to be dreamed up and marketed out of attics in towns which are located on direct plane routes to places such as Costa Rica, the Bahamas, or Liechtenstein. *Never, never, never invest in a tax shelter where the promoter is headquartered outside the United States. Period. Extradition is very difficult these days.*

(6) If the promoter constantly stresses the tax advantage of his deal, consider endowing your favorite charity instead.

8.

The (T)axman Cometh

You may not think so, but the Internal Revenue Service has a sense of humor. Or at least some of the actions the Service (as it's called by its employees) took during and after the reign of Jerome Kurtz (appointed commissioner by President Carter) have been, if not downright hilarious, then at the very least, sardonically tongue-in-cheek.

I mean, what can you say about a tax collection agency which hires as one of its press aides someone with the distinctly intimidating name of Tony Bombardieri? The fact that Mr. Bombardieri is a veritable pussycat is much beside the point. Talk about sending in the heavy guns!

In the same period of time, the Service came out with a series of rulings and opinions which have punched rather large holes in some absolutely hysterical tax shelters, and has done so on dates which had to have been selected by some inscrutable auditor with an eye for the macabre.

The first of these rulings came on October 31, 1977, a date now known in tax shelter circles as The Halloween Massacre. These little interpretations by Kurtz's Killers effectively ended the major attractions of coal, timber, and master recording deals. Such shelters used leverage to boost up-front royalties to landowners and recording artists, royalties which in many cases were based on inflated fair market values, and which were rarely delivered in the form of cash. Government bond straddles (which mercifully fizzled before any of us journalists had time to figure them out) and completed older movie deals were also affected by the massacre.

The Christmas Eve Garrote took place in 1979, when the *IRS Bulletin,* dated December 24th, took out after people who were playing a new twist on the old charitable deduction game. This was a scheme very much in vogue during the latter part of the decade, and still lurking around today. Usually, an investor would buy a rare or priceless commodity—old bibles, gems, artbooks— and hold it for a year. Then, he or she would turn around and donate it to a charitable institution and take the deduction based on the inflated retail, or collector's, price. The Christmas Eve Garrote dealt with donations of exotic plants, and was a wondrously written example of Ebenezer Scroogism which left the taxpayer in question as exposed and abused as Bob Cratchit.

Immediately afterward, the Service came through with the earthshaking New Year's Eve Slaughter. This ruling, on December 31, 1979, was aimed specifically at tax shelters in lithographs of signed, limited editions from famous contemporary artists. These deals are simply chock-full of wonderfully impossible details which we'll get into later on in this book. This ruling, however, was based on an IRS interpretation of the fair market value of such lithographs, and this decision was reached with the help of independent art appraisers whom the IRS called in for the purposes of backing up its own suspicions. Undaunted, artwork promoters are still peddling these deals all over the country. One told me that the New Year's Eve Slaughter was "a scare tactic by the IRS. Instead of selling $30 million this year, we only sold $20 million." Ahem.

Then there were the St. Patrick's Day Murders in 1980. This edition of the *IRS Bulletin* contained seven adverse rulings on tax shelters, ranging from oil drilling to mining to charitable contributions to advance royalties. These were neat little snippets which had the effect of once more reminding those interested parties that the IRS is truly getting its act together when it comes to cracking down on "abusive and egregious tax shelters."

Well, the word is out. But the question remains: How seriously should an individual take the IRS in an era when Tax Court rulings seem to contradict each other, people are escaping taxation altogether in the underground economy, and the IRS, by its own admission, is woefully understaffed?

The answer when it comes to tax shelters is: as seriously as Mom's apple pie, Ronald Reagan notwithstanding.

Please understand that I do not wish to imply that one should take a cavalier attitude toward the power of the IRS to disrupt one's life. *Au contraire,* I take these people very seriously for the very fact that if they do choose to come after you, and you're in the right all the way down the line, the emotional experience you have to

go through to prove you're correct is enough to trauma-
tize even the most laid-back coupon-clipper from Laguna
Beach.

It should not be lost upon you that the one agency
which has had more success nailing gangsters, murder-
ers, and philandering politicians has been the IRS—the
court of last resort in this country. One should have a
healthy respect for these boys and girls, especially when
it comes to tax shelters.

But one should also understand the IRS's limita-
tions. This is a mighty big country, with all sorts of
strange things happening all over the place. There is
every reason to believe that each year, despite its careful
monitoring of public deals, the Service misses a few
frauds here and there. They even fall victim to the old
left-hand-not-knowing-what-the-right-hand-is-doing
scenario when it comes to interagency squabbles with
the Securities and Exchange Commission. They lose
their fair share of challenges in the Tax Courts as well.
But Kurtz made a start toward uncovering consistent
patterns of abuse. "We're not out to knock legitimate
tax shelters," notes a member of the Service's recently
created 16-person Tax Shelter Committee, which ferrets
out new twists on old themes and applies the screws ac-
cordingly. "But we are concerned that abusive shelters
undermine the confidence people should have in the
system as a whole."

This is all straightforward enough, but the question
still remains, "How much of a chance do I have of getting nailed with an audit if I invest in a tax shelter of any
kind, let alone an 'abusive' one?" The answer seems to be
"Pretty good," especially if the Service latches on to
what it considers to be a trend, and programs its computers properly, or goes headhunting for everyone who's
in the deal.

Recently, the courts held that the IRS has the right to ask a promoter for the names of all the investors in a given deal (even if it's set up as a series of sole proprietorships on a private-placement basis), if the Service has reason to believe that abuses may have occurred. While some view this as a license for the IRS to go on a witch hunt, others—especially those with the IRS, and they're the ones who count—feel that a legitimate deal offered by legitimate people with solid economic chance for success is likely to be considered as just another investment by the Service's computer; but those which stretch the limits of the Tax Code, and one's sense of humor (or the absurd), deserve to be scrutinized.

Yet, people fall constantly for this too-good-to-be-true baloney, preferring to listen to glib, sweet-talking salespersons rather than following their own common sense about business viability, and instincts about what constitutes an abusive tax shelter. Our friend Fred and The Razor in Chapter Five was a good example, and hardly atypical. There are thousands and thousands of other cases. It all boils down to a question of what kind of person you are. If you're reasonably responsible, believe in a sense of fair play, have an outlook on life which takes such things as ethics into consideration—and most of all, if you believe that "Everything Catches Up To You In The End"—you'll pick a shelter which should cause you few tax nightmares. If, on the other hand, you're a son of a bitch or just plain stupid to begin with, you get what you deserve.

The plain fact is that the IRS is under tremendous pressure—from Congress, the commissioner, the executive branch, and from some segments of the public—to improve its methods of tax collection on all fronts. There is widespread tax evasion in this country, with up to 20% of the Gross National Product by some estimates going untaxed in transactions which are carried out off-the-books. There are thousands of tax shelters organized each year, however, which are not off-the-books. It stands to reason that the IRS is going to be much more effective checking out what it can see (tax returns) than what it can't (cash and barter). Thus, you can pretty much count on the fact that if you play cutesy with the Tax Code—and you leave a paper trail behind you—the computer will nail you long before some bureaucrat up-stairs has figured out the latest scam. Therein lies the rub in tax shelters when it comes to the IRS—the tax-man might not get you, but his little machine will.

The *IRS Bulletin*, issued each week, is a good place to look for trends in the Service's thinking about tax shelters. This boring little pamphlet regularly sum-marizes "rulings" made by the Service on various cases brought to its attention (either by investors, the com-puter, the grapevine, or personal vendetta). These rul-ings are the IRS's interpretations of regulations in the Tax Code and, as such, carry no force of law. In fact, a ruling is merely a position which the IRS has to defend, and these rulings can be challenged in court either by the party who was the subject of the ruling, or any other party who is crazy enough to do so. The Halloween Massacre, Christmas Eve Garrote, New Year's Eve Slaughter, and St. Patrick's Day Murders all appeared as rulings in the *Bulletin*. In effect, these rulings caught people in the act, putting the damper on many of the types of shelters in question, if only because few people want to go to the expense, or personal exposure, of challenging the IRS in court. A better reason, of course, is that the Service is usually pretty sure its position will hold up in court when it publishes a ruling in the *Bulletin*, and most tax experts know that. When the IRS issues an unfavorable ruling, notes newsletter publisher Bill Brennan, "the investor will pay."

Most of these rulings over the past few years have hardly affected the legitimate tax shelters. In almost every case, the rulings have been aimed at the credibility stretchers, the kinds of deals where everybody makes out except the government. Remember, the purpose of a tax shelter is not to screw the government; it's to get Uncle Sam to assume part of the risk of underwriting a business venture with you. You play it his way, he'll generally leave you alone. There's plenty of opportunity to get Uncle Sam into a position of benign neglect without running the risk that he'll be looking over your shoulder every step of the way.

The rest of this book will show you the best strategies to consider in order to plan a reasonable tax shelter portfolio, one which gives you a good chance of economic success, gives you tax advantages, and keeps the Service off your neck.

Part Three

Real Estate: Remember, Ice Cream Melts...

9.

The Syndicate Is
Out To Get You . . .

If the decade of the 1970s has left any economic legacy in its quivering wake, it's the assumption that any investment in real estate automatically leads to a bountiful pot of the glittering stuff at the end of the rainbow. True, there are plenty of millionaires lounging around the shores of Southern California, ordinary people who had the prescience when they were thrown out of work during the 1974-75 recession to take the real estate exams and cash in on the slightly insane boom which occurred along the San Andreas fault shortly thereafter.

And, true, there are dozens of books you can buy which point to all the advantages of real estate as an investment, inflation hedge, tax shelter, and security blanket—books written by people who made some money in the field and are now reaping large royalties on the sales of their books.

Will Rogers may have advised his contemporaries to buy land because God isn't making any more of it, but judging from the way real estate has turned over during the past few years, one would think that syndicators and promoters have found an endless supply of office buildings, shopping centers, apartment complexes, condos, industrial parks, mini warehouse developments, and the occasional hybrid parcel to keep the nation's appetite for land and its by-products satiated. Real estate has become the next best thing to ice cream in America. Unfortunately, if you're not careful, you will find that ice cream can melt all over your best suit. Real estate won't necessarily melt (Mt. St. Helens notwithstanding), but real estate deals have a tendency to crumble at precisely the most inopportune times.

When it comes to tax shelters, those which deal with real estate are probably the most popular these days. One reason, of course, is the wildly escalating retail market for the stuff during the past few years, a market which can, and did, turn soft in many areas of the country with the onset of the recessions of 1980 and 1981-82. The key factor to keep in mind about real estate is that yes, it appreciates, usually in direct proportion to the rise in the rate of inflation; but it's the *depreciation* which really counts when you talk about the tax possibilities, and the chance for sheltered income.

The most important reason why real estate has survived as our most popular tax shelter has to do with the fact that it is the only industry left unscathed by the at-risk provisions of the Tax Reform Act of 1976, the Revenue Act of 1978, and ERTA. As you recall, the at-risk rules specify that an investor cannot deduct more than the amount invested—the amount at risk—without being liable to pay off the leverage. You can sign non-recourse notes, and take the resulting deductions for interest and depreciation in a real estate investment where you cannot in other tax shelters.

Why this merciful treatment of real estate? Enter the Sacred Cow Theory and, if you will, a bit of cynicism. Real estate is a very powerful ingredient in the brew which goes into the capitalist cauldron. And, it's also a subject which hits very close to home on Capitol Hill. In the days when Congresspersons by the scores owned oil wells or farms, the tax deductions for such ventures withstood the reform assault rather handily. As those legislators retired or died, they were replaced by Congresspersons whose main source of net worth, or a good portion of their personal assets, was tied up in their homes or other real estate. Since Congress makes the tax laws, what got reformed were the investments which were carried to the grave; what is allowed to continue to escape the reformers' knives is real estate, because very few Congresspersons have been known to enjoy cutting their own throats.

Another reason real estate has gained such widespread popularity in the past decade is the fact that Wall Street has discovered it, and has instituted a high-powered marketing campaign for selling a wide cross section of their customers' interests in various types of real estate syndicates. With the small investor becoming increasingly wary about the stocks and bonds markets, there was a natural tendency on the part of Wall Street (which survives by pushing products and generating commissions) to seek out a new and exciting form of investment for the average person to sink some dough into. Hence, an increasingly large share of the private placement business—besides all the public market—in real estate syndications has been gobbled up by investment firms of all sizes and shapes.

Working in concert with a handful of major real estate promoters, property managers, and speculators, the boys and girls on the Street have come up with syndicates which offer either income and little tax shelter, or good tax shelter and little income, or some which offer

scant hope of any tax or investment salvation. The
public market for these investments now exceeds $1
billion annually, with the private placements certainly
adding up to a similar amount, according to Steve
Roulac of the *Real Estate Syndication Report,* an excellent monthly review of the field which is published by
Questor Associates, San Francisco.

There are a number of arguments for and against investments in real estate syndications which come out of
large Wall Street firms; but by and large, if you're looking for a good tax shelter syndicate with a chance to
generate up-front deductions, partially sheltered income
for several years, and strong upside potential for capital
gains down the road, you would be well advised to be
careful about plunging into a large, nationwide syndicate. Here are some reasons.

Of all the tax shelter investments you can make, real
estate is the one which is most sensitive to the nature of
man. It is, therefore, the one tax shelter which requires
intensive analysis of demographics, marketing, economic trends, and the fickleness of particular segments
of the American public. Real estate management requires thorough knowledge of specific markets because
trends in the industry are much more localized than in
other tax shelters. For example, there was a boom in real
estate in Atlanta in the early 1970s; in New York City at
the same time, real estate was a total disaster area. By
1977, however, the situation had completely reversed.

You don't have the same volatility in other tax
shelters. In oil and gas, you know there's a ready market
for whatever comes out of the ground, and the variables
you're subject to are the competence of the driller and
the willingness of the earth to give up its fossilized matter. You can say the same about other energy shelters as
well. Intelligent study of the capital spending plans and
production needs of business and industry will generally

lead to reasonable conclusions for certain kinds of equipment needed on a national, or international, level. When it comes to farming tax shelters, well, people have to eat, and you're sometimes subject to the whims of Mother Nature, or government controls. And unless you've got a trainer who pumps drugs into your nags, your investment in horses boils down to elements which are basically beyond the control of mankind—genetics, good lungs, brittle legs.

In real estate, however, all it takes is the wrong location to put a multimillion dollar, architecturally stunning building into bankruptcy. *A human error.* Real estate is subject to more human errors—and human fraud—than almost any other tax shelter. It requires enormous human effort to manage multiple properties, and above all else, an investment in any tax shelter is an investment in management. The sad fact is that despite the tremendous strides made in property management techniques during the past decade, there is still a shortage of competent, motivated, highly trained property managers around these days. The best ones concentrate on managing in their own backyard—and therein lies one of the big rubs when it comes to nationally syndicated real estate investments.

Most of the deals coming out of major Wall Street firms involve ownership of property in several areas of the country. Usually, there is a mix of properties—shopping centers, office buildings, garden apartments. While promoters will tell you that a good geographic and property mix is necessary to soften the downside risks of regional economic slowdowns, there is also the question of spreading one's management capability too thinly. Because real estate is an intensely personal activity, requiring careful attention to detail and cooperation from everyone from janitors to owner, it is difficult to imagine how a syndicate which raises $50 million to buy buildings of various sizes and descriptions in Los

Angeles, Atlanta, Dallas, Phoenix, Tulsa, and Kalama-
zoo can expect to balance all the balls well enough to
keep everyone happy, investors included.

One thing for certain is that the owners who sell
property to these syndicates will be happy, because they
are probably getting top dollar (or more) for their buildings. Why? Look, it can take from 90 to 180 days between the time a syndicate makes an offer, puts down
earnest money (if any), draws up a prospectus, sends it
off to the SEC, convinces Wall Street to take on the deal,
signs up all the investors, and then *closes the deal* (at
which time money changes hands). If you were the owner
of such property, and had to wait up to six months for
your money, how would that affect the price? Wouldn't
you hedge your bet upwards to adjust for future inflation and the possibility that the deal might fall through
(in which case you'd keep the deposit based on the inflated price)? What happens when five or six owners sell
to a large syndicate and take the same attitude? Right.
The investor runs the risk of overpaying, thereby reducing income potential. Of course, overpaying could
generate bigger tax write-offs, but there are problems
here as well, as we shall see.

On the other hand, there are syndications offered by
Wall Street firms, financial and estate planners, attorneys, CPAs, and experienced entrepreneurs which
carefully restrict their activities to one or two properties
in a local area. Some of these deals have decent tax
shelter and good income, can be offered on a public or
private basis and, in many cases, represent true opportunities for large capital gains down the road. The best
deals are those wherein a syndicate manages to pick up
prime property at below the market price because the
owner may be overextended on other deals, and may be
willing to settle for a smaller profit in order to generate
some quick cash. (Private deals of this sort can close
almost overnight.)

One deal which impressed this observer came about as a result of an estate planning firm putting 20 of its clients together to purchase an office building in New York City for $1.8 million, and then converting it into a commercial condominium for upwards of $9 million. Deals like this are tough to find, especially on a public basis, but they are available if you keep your ears to the ground and open your mouth discreetly. Of course, the private deals are where the cute tax tricks can occur, and you should have some sophisticated tax advice from your CPA or attorney before committing yourself. This is not to say that the public deals are tax-cleansed, although there are fewer chances of tripping a red flag in the IRS computer with a public deal. However, both public and private real estate deals have been known to use one of the more questionable tax gimmicks which can get you into deep tax trouble if you're not careful: the wraparound mortgage.

Here's how a wraparound works: John Doe Associates buys an apartment complex in 1979 for $1.5 million, taking out a $1.2 million mortgage at 9¼% from a bank. In 1981, it sells the complex to a limited partnership for $3 million with no down payment, but takes a 12% non-recourse note from the partners. The note is secured by the complex. That gives the partners more of a depreciation deduction—$3 million as opposed to $1.5 million. What's more, the up-front interest deduction they can theoretically take will also be boosted because they haven't paid a bit of principal yet. John Doe collects the money in installments, taking a fee to manage the property (also deductible), while paying off its 9¼% mortgage to the bank.

The problem is that the IRS may step in and claim that the property's fair market value is closer to $2 million than $3 million. Zap. This would directly affect the depreciation based on $3 million and may affect the interest deductions based on the 12% rate on the $3 million as well. A smart investor will know these numbers can mean trouble ahead, especially if the cash flow from the complex is barely enough to cover expenses based on a 9¼% mortgage rate on a $1.5 million price. Real estate appreciates in value, but not at the expense of cash flow.

Other tax wrinkles to be leery of include the buying out of one limited partnership by another—which can lead to questions of who gets what loss when. This usually occurs when one partnership bails out another one that's suffering financial difficulties. The troubled partnership may subordinate its losses to the new partners. While that sounds good, the IRS may step in and nix it all by claiming that there's no economic justification for those losses because the cash flow to either or both partnerships may be negligible—or nonexistent. *Remember, a tax shelter can legitimately generate huge write-offs only if it can show the IRS that there's a reasonable chance of making money eventually.* You'd be wise to get a smart real estate advisor to look over these "ice cream deals" in advance.

The best kind of real estate tax shelter is the one which you set up for yourself, or go into with a few other investors, under the management of a sharp property expert, in a well-located commercial or residential building in your own home town. There are literally hundreds of deals which can be structured, from buying a condo and renting it out to renovating a loft building and turning it into apartments. But these deals require careful attention to detail, and are not for everyone, especially armchair investors. If you're the hands-on type, you will have to spend a good deal of time reading, taking extension courses, and going into the business of real estate for yourself—or hiring someone you totally trust to handle your portfolio. If you're enamored about the possibilities of real estate, but bored with the prospects of management, you are simply going to have to consider a larger project, and those are the syndications we're concerned about in this book.

Here are some specific *caveats* to be aware of when it comes to sizing up the potential of a large syndication—in addition, of course, to the general guidelines detailed in Chapter Seven:

• Be wary if there's a provision for fees to be paid by the limited partners to the seller for covenants restricting the seller from competing. The IRS may rule that these fees are not deductible, and this could be a tip-off of general poor tax strategy in the deal.

• Be alert to conflicts-of-interest, especially if there are all sorts of "affiliated" companies handling various aspects of the deal. You should try to determine whether the deal could have been put together without any conflicts. For example, would an independent real estate broker have been able to acquire the proposed properties at a lower price than a broker who's affiliated with the company? That may well be the case if the promoter or an affiliated party had an interest in that property.

• The prospectus should list the properties the partnership will invest in—locations, purchase prices, cash flow, depreciation schedules, and rates of return. There has been a proliferation of blind-pool syndicates of late (illegal, by the way, in New York State), wherein the promoter states that after raising the money, he'll go out and buy the best properties available and close immediately, thereby eliminating the risk of overpaying because of long delays involved in the registration process. This is a valid argument—but only to the extent that the promoter involved has a long and excellent track record operating in a similar fashion. Generally, these deals are structured more for those seeking immediate income, rather than tax shelter, because a prospectus which doesn't list properties in advance cannot

effectively disclose the tax write-offs one should expect.
If you run into a deal which is a blind-pool *tax shelter* (as
opposed to a blind-pool *income syndicate*), and the prospectus lists the tax deductions you're going to get, ask
the promoter whether he's going to have to scramble all
over the place to match buildings to his projections, or
whether he's got the properties all lined up. If he has to
scramble, the promoter may indeed scramble—to Costa
Rica. If he's got the property lined up, why wasn't it disclosed in the prospectus?

    • Always look at the assumptions behind the num-
bers—they're often very important. Look closely at the
specific properties the partnership will buy to find out
how well-built and managed they are. Look at costs and
rental demand. If the deal doesn't make economic sense,
all the tax benefits may be a pipe dream.

    • Since you want a deal which lists properties to be
acquired, you should expect to get some return on investment at the end of the first quarter of the year after
the partnership is activated—except, of course, in new
construction deals, wherein you would expect to get a
specific timetable of rent-up and occupancy dates. The
property you acquire is *yours*, and you should start getting some cash back as soon as possible.

    • Make sure you can get the tax deductions you
need in the year you need them. You can't get the write-
off until the money is spent by the promoter. Many real
estate deals offered late in the year may not close until
after December 31, so you may get no write-off when you
need it. Similarly, deals which close in the last quarter
and take tax deductions for the whole year may be subject to IRS scrutiny, and much of those deductions may
be disallowed.

    • Find out the depreciation the partnership plans to
take on its properties. Accelerated depreciation, which is

still available on some types of properties, may boost the up-front deductions, but may also be recaptured when the properties are eventually sold. That means you'll have to pay income tax on the difference between accelerated depreciation and straight-line depreciation if the building is sold within a set number of years. Straight-line depreciation reduces the up-front tax advantages, but it also will not trigger the 15% minimum preference tax which accelerated depreciation can set off.

• If the General Partner has the power to sell the properties acquired by the partnership—and has equity in the deal—he or she shouldn't get commissions on any sales until the limited partners have received all the money they have put into the deal as well as a stated return on investment. Why should the General Partner get something off the top before you get something for your bottom line?

• Shy away from the deal if real estate is combined with any other business (equipment leasing, coal mining), simply to take advantage of the up-front real estate deductions. You may not be sure of what business you're investing in, and neither, alas, might the promoter.

10.

Apartments:
Beyond The Valley
Of The Numbers

Let's say you've decided that as far as investments in
real estate are concerned, nothing can beat multifamily
apartment complexes. After all, there's a growing demand for housing—what with the SSWDs taking over
the country (Single, Separated, Widowed, Divorced), and
the highly mobile nature of the American consumer.
There is a powerful host of factors on your side of this
argument, notwithstanding the fact that in times of
economic slowdown, apartment complexes have been
hurt by tenant skip-outs or defaults on rent payments.
There are literally thousands of complexes, ranging from
garden-type to high-rise to low-rise, coming on the
market each year, many of which have been depreciated
out by their current owners (always a valid reason for
selling), others simply because they're turkeys and no
one wants to live there.

How do you get a handle on whether or not a specific apartment house deal is best for you? It's not easy. You've got to get out your manager's hard hat and dig beneath the balance sheets. Cash flow and rate-of-return figures listed in a prospectus might not be the easiest, or best, source of reliable information. Nor will comparing similar properties in a given city. That's because variables such as location, design, physical plant, tenant mix, age of the building, lease schedules, utility arrangements, resident manager idiosyncrasies, and sometimes even the weather all must be analyzed to optimize your return on an apartment complex investment. Here are some points to keep in mind when scouting around for residential properties:

Know Thy Neighbor: Become absolutely familiar with the demographics of the neighborhood an apartment complex is located in before investing your money. This is critical if the syndicate has properties located in other parts of the country (one more reason to stay as close to home as possible). For example, there are many good-looking complexes available in Los Angeles, Atlanta, Birmingham, Oklahoma City, Austin, Houston—you name the city, something's for sale. But the question to ask is: *Where* in Los Angeles, Atlanta, Birmingham, Oklahoma City, Austin, or Houston? The answer can often mean the difference between steady, dependable tenants and quick turnover or skip-outs. Fancy four-color brochures with pretty pictures might camouflage many a tale of management and fiscal woe. While an investor in a large syndicate cannot be expected to check out construction, lay of the land, and intangibles such as carpeting, leaders and gutters and washing machine cycles in each complex listed in the deal, there are some ways to check out the tangibles of a deal to counterbalance the intangible projections:

1. Check the rent rolls against bank deposits for the previous 18 months (the promoter should have a copy of

this data on file; if not, he's not a good potential manager). Also, take a close look at a detailed lease-expiration list for each tenant. While some managers point to the fact that short leases are good because rents can be raised quicker, this can also lead to constant vacancy problems—especially in the case of highly transient tenants attracted to studio or one-bedroom complexes. If this is so, find a better deal elsewhere. Marketing and maintenance costs tend to get out of hand in a complex where there's high turnover.

2. Laundry facilities in each apartment are better than common-use facilities. That's especially true in these energy conscious days when tenants pay for their own utilities. Replacement and maintenance costs can be dramatically reduced, and rents can be scaled higher, when such amenities are included.

3. Become a potential tenant. Visit the rental office of the complex yourself (or, in the case of a large deal with many complexes, choose one city, take a trip, and write off the costs). Then, visit the competition. Listen to the sales pitch you get in each place, inspect the available apartments (not the models), ask important consumer-oriented questions which can have a direct effect on rentals, hence, cash flow into your pocket. How often will the apartment be painted? Who pays for appliance repairs? Is security adequate? How close are necessary shopping facilities, gas stations, public transportation? By comparison shopping, you should be able to answer the big question: Would you want to live there yourself? If not, keep shopping for another deal.

We've all heard horror stories of investments which have gone down the tubes, but how many have you heard with all the gruesome details laid out for examination? Here's a case history of one apartment complex which reveals many potential bugaboos. Granted, this project is an extreme, but any of its all-too-common defects could affect the cash flow and rate-of-return on any deal.

Aquarian Ridge is a 26-building garden apartment complex in a metro area in the booming Sunbelt. It was purchased by a limited partnership at bargain basement prices because the seller was overextended and needed to consolidate his activities. The purchase price was an assumption of mortgages on the property by a group of investors who had to put no money down to get into the deal.

The General Partner was an experienced management company headquartered in the same city with a long track record of sound apartment management. However, most of the experience was in government-subsidized housing. This was the General Partner's first venture into a conventionally financed, luxury apartment project. Most of the limited partners had been investors in previous deals organized over the years by the General Partner. It was, to say the least, the perfect set-up.

Aquarian Ridge contained an equal number of one and two-bedroom apartments. The two-bedroom units were spectacular duplexes. Physically, the complex was a gem—on the surface, at least. Bordering a natural lake (which, alas, had a tendency to turn green with algae buildup, but nevertheless, a lake it was) on rolling, wooded terrain, the buildings had natural wood exteriors, flat, mansard-like roofs, large carpeted rooms, a central laundry facility, clubhouse and swimming pool. In addition, it was surrounded by two other brand-new complexes, mostly two and three-bedroom units, in a growing area of town. Rents were very reasonable: $225 a month for a one-bedroom unit, and $305 for two bedrooms. Each apartment was separately metered for utilities. Occupancy rates had fluctuated between 75% and 90% for two years. Rental income was estimated at $300,000 per year.

The deal went belly-up in 12 months.

Mistake Number One: Location. Aquarian Ridge was located near the airport, on a direct flight path for night flights. While this location was ideal for airline employees, frequent transfers of flight attendants—and just plain noise—led to a good many early lease terminations. Turnover was almost constant. The other complexes surrounding the lake were also affected, but they were not on a direct path to the runways. And since they had more bedrooms, they tended to attract airport personnel who had children (and remained put longer) or singles who could easily replace roommates.

Before long, an undesirable element began taking over the available apartments at Aquarian Ridge, which led to police raids of allegedly nefarious activities. Let's just say that the three P's—pimps, prostitutes, and pill-pushers—had taken over. One would think the bad publicity didn't help the rental situation.

The location was also in the wrong part of town for shopping. The management wanted to attract chic, free-spending airline workers. However, those people, it turned out, preferred to commute further to the airport so that they could live closer to centrally located stores and the night life. Public transportation, although available, was inadequate. Hence, an automobile became an essential expense for most tenants.

Aquarian Ridge was six years old, and had been solidly rented in its early stages because it was the first in the area. Wear-and-tear on carpeting, drapes, physical plant, and laundry facilities, however, necessitated expensive replacement by the time the new partnership took over. In addition, the natural wood siding on the buildings, while useful in certain sections of the country and certainly aesthetic, buckled and molded in this city because of its high humidity and heavy annual rainfall. The dew from the green lake certainly didn't help, either.

The weather played havoc with the roofing. Because the roofs were flat, the run-off through leaders and gutters was not efficient. In addition, falling leaves from the trees in autumn (even in the Sunbelt, leaves can fall) clogged the leaders and gutters constantly. Hence, roofs started to buckle and leak, leading to costly repairs; leaders and gutters had to be replaced; and there was water damage to some apartment interiors, not covered by normal insurance.

Another rude shock: The project's useful life had to be compromised by poor dredging of the land around the lake, resulting in uneven settling of buildings and pavement. To bring matters to a macabre nadir, it was discovered that during the project's first year, one of the buildings fronting the lake *actually slid into the water* after a week-long rain. The building was hauled out of the lake, and the developer simply put up another one in its place!

The management hired outside construction consultants to head off future embarrassment, and to get the complex in more desirable shape—so that it could be rented up, or sold off. All of these problems led to a severe cash flow crisis. After repairs were made, attempts were made to rectify the situation with heavy promotion based on discounted rents. Even a name change to Camelot-on-the-Lake didn't work. Camelot-*nee*-Aquarian had, in effect, lived a useful life for as long as it possibly could, and was not only depreciated out, but played out as well.

While this horror story is not typical, it does point out the problems which can come up in managing a large complex of buildings in a single location in a city which is well-known by the General Partner, and which on paper looks like a great buy.

11.

Section 8s And Other Government Fantasies

Never underestimate Uncle Sam's desire to be one of the boys. He figures that since everyone and his brother and sister are into real estate, it must be a good deal, so, why not join in all the fun? Except that when he joined the game, he brought along his own ball, and his own rules.

Back in the late 1960s and early 1970s, the Federal Government encouraged thousands of shelter-seeking taxpayers to plunge their capital into housing projects primarily designed for the poor and lower-income denizens of this country. These were the storied FHA Section 236 and 221(d)(3) projects (among other numbers) which generally took the form of sterile-looking apartment complexes in economically depressed neighborhoods, primarily throughout the Sunbelt. Those were the halcyon days of get-rich-quick promoters who managed to do all the right paperwork quickly, then syndicate their private deals through brokerage firm networks which were only too happy to jump on the *pro bono publico* bandwagon in exchange for commissions, the latter of which were diminishing in the face of investor disenchantment with the equity markets.

Well, you know what happened to many of those FHA projects: They not only fell prey to mismanagement and sometimes outright fraud on the part of the promoter/developers (which led to bankruptcies galore), but they also hardly provided decent housing for the underprivileged classes. In many cases, they were instant slums, just add Uncle Sam's water in the form of mortgage subsidies and other enticing goodies.

Now we've got Section 8s. Strange how the government manages to come up with macabre appellations for some of its more questionable programs, eh? Section 8s are not designed as housing projects for the less balanced of our military personnel. Rather, it refers to a program of the Department of Housing and Urban Development created to subsidize the rents of lower income families in projects which are supposed to provide decent housing. The twist on this program is that the promoter has the option of building housing for several classes of tenants—including a provision which allows restriction of the apartments to elderly citizens.

Don't get me wrong. I'm all for decent housing for those who are being squeezed out of the market by inflation and the speculative greed of high-rolling real estate developers who feel the world is populated only by people who can afford to pay $1,200 for a one-bedroom bare bones apartment 12 miles from the nearest supermarket. But the problem with Section 8s, or any government housing program, is the inherent cynicism built into the system. The government feels it has a responsibility to provide housing for those who can't afford it. Yet it hasn't the guts to do this in a manner which might appeal to those with the biggest stake in that housing—the people who will live there. So, tax incentives for high-tax bracket investors are built into the projects in order to attract capital from the private sector. Unfortunately, these tax incentives open the way for so many abuses that another element of the government, the Internal

Revenue Service, often steps in and negates the very incentives built into the program in the first place. In addition, the government often places so many economic restrictions on these deals that rarely, if ever, does anyone make any money except, of course, the promoters, who charge large fees for the investors to become limited partners.

It all boils down to the concept of the free lunch. Uncle Sam wants a free lunch because he doesn't want the responsibility of owning and managing real estate, but wants the credit for providing "decent housing" for the less fortunate. Investors want a free lunch in the form of high up-front tax write-offs and a chance to say that they're doing something good for society. Stockbrokers want a free lunch in the form of commissions, but no responsibility if the deal goes sour. And the promoters, well, there is every reason to believe that they are the only ones who don't ever have to pay for dining at Uncle Sam's pig-out.

Does it sound like I'm totally against federal housing projects? No, I'm not. It's just that the human motivations of greed have fewer reins on them when all the wonderful plums are tossed at them by Uncle Sam. It's a nasty bit of business, and here's why.

Under Section 8 of the U.S. Housing Act of 1937, the Department of Housing and Urban Development (HUD) makes up the difference between what a lower income household can afford for rent (no more than 25% of adjusted income) and what the fair market value for an apartment is determined to be. The housing is in either new or substantially rehabilitated buildings. Rehabilitations qualify as "new in use" buildings. They can be depreciated faster over a shorter period of time as newly built projects under the first-user provisions of the IRS Code, Section 167(k). Already we've got finagling.

HUD bases its eligibility requirements for tenants on the following oft-misinterpreted statement: "Tenants must be lower income households with incomes amounting to 80% of the area median income or less." This is a very loaded sentence.

Some promoters claim that the 80% formula will allow tenants with reasonably high incomes to qualify for Section 8 assistance. After all, if the median income for Mythical County is $21,000, it might be assumed that a working couple earning $16,800 would be eligible to live in such a project. That's partially correct. They can live there, but *without* HUD rent-subsidy assistance. That's because another wrinkle to the 80% formula now comes in: The number of people in a household determines the maximum allowable gross income HUD will allow for rental assistance. Thus, an annual income of $16,800 may qualify a *family of eight* to live in a Section 8 project in Mythical County. For a working couple, the maximum gross income allowed might be closer to $10,000, which, unless you're illegal aliens working in a sweatshop, is fairly easy to exceed in these days of high inflation. Once the gross income is exceeded (people get raises, and second incomes must be included), the tenant loses the right to a HUD subsidy, and must pay the full fair market value for that apartment. In effect, this keeps Section 8 housing restricted to people who cannot break out of the poverty cycle—*or cannot afford to*. At best, it can lead to fraud on the part of the tenants. At worst, if the tenants are honest, what you may suddenly discover is that after a couple of years, turnover in the apartments gets so great that vacancies keep occurring, and cash flow back to the investors stops. How can this happen?

Let's say a Section 8 project has one-third of its tenants on the marginal income line. After a year or so, some of those tenants become ineligible to receive the HUD subsidy. Now, let's say one of those tenants is that

$10,000 working couple who can only afford $2,500 per year (25% of their income, by the HUD guidelines, or $208 per month) for their one-bedroom apartment. Suddenly, the husband gets a raise, the wife gets a job, and their income jumps to $18,000. Let's also say that their one-bedroom apartment has been judged to have a *fair market value* of $450 per month. OK, they lose their subsidy, and their rent more than doubles to $5,400 per year. Taking into consideration their higher tax bracket, this couple is now *worse off* earning *more money*. What are their options? Well, they could neglect to report the increased income, but when the inspectors come around to look at their tax records, that could be tough to explain. Or, they could look at each other and say: "Hey, we're moving up, we're making more money, but we still have to live in a poor neighborhood and pay uptown rents. We're moving out." It's a plausible twist on the lyrics of Billy Joel's hit song, "Movin' Out":

"If that's movin' up/Then I'm movin' out."*

OK, you don't care about all this business of what *can* happen. What you want to know is how Section 8s work, and assuming you can find a good deal, what you're likely to gain in the form of tax advantages. To be sure, there are some promoters and nonprofit organizations who have established decent living conditions for tenants and seem to work out equitable up-front tax breaks for investors which do not run a high risk of IRS scrutiny. But they are few and far between, and all the tips listed in previous chapters about checking out promoters and deals apply double to Section 8 promoters. Why? It's a simple case of commitment and economics. It can often take up to two years of tedious site selection, paperwork, meetings with community groups and bureaucrats before a developer has received all the necessary commitments to get his deal underway. If the developer is a specialist in Section 8s and other government-assisted projects, more than likely he's been able

---

* Joelsongs (BMI), *The Stranger*, Columbia Records, 1977.

to keep his business going on the success of his projects.
A developer who decides to branch out into Section 8s
more than likely is making his money from nongovern-
ment projects which require his primary attention; a Section 8 may be an interesting sideline which offers a good
opportunity to make up-front profits on fees, and keeps
some of his staff busy during times of slowdowns in the
conventionally financed real estate business.

In any case, after a developer has gone through all
the trouble of putting a deal together, he's set to raise
equity from investors against the preliminary mortgage
commitments granted by his lenders. This is where the
investor comes in. You're most likely to be approached
by someone who believes you're looking for a big tax
shelter. That's because the up-front write-offs on a Section 8 deal can exceed two or three times your cash investment. In terms of pure tax shelter, then, Section 8s
offer the biggest write-offs in town right now, and they
are very hot on Wall Street.

Under Section 8, the difference between what HUD
determines to be the fair market value for the apartment
and the rent owed by the tenant is paid directly to the
project's owners (the limited partnership formed by the
promoter) by HUD. The tenant executes a separate lease
with the owner for his share of the rent. Hence, if a project's annual rent roll is $300,000, and the combined
rents owed by tenants amounted to only $180,000, HUD
would pay the landlord $120,000 in rent subsidies.

Questions about how fair market value rent levels
are fixed are usually settled between HUD and the promoter. Each project is different, and each must pass certain basic criteria before construction can begin. These
criteria, when met, assure that HUD will enter into a
contract to provide rent subsidies for 20 to 40 years.
Thus, even if Congress or HUD terminates the Section 8
program in the future (and there are rumblings of this

sort), the government is under contract to continue subsidies. In addition, tenants are obligated to pay utilities under the separate metering provisions of Section 8.

The deal can be attractive because HUD will help owners out during the rent-up period—in case times are tough. HUD will pay the rent for unoccupied apartments for the first two months, plus the principal and interest costs for unoccupied apartments for the next 12 months. To top it off, HUD will let a landlord automatically raise rents every year and will even grant emergency rent increases if costs start soaring. But generally speaking, when these projects first open, there are long waiting lines for these apartments because the government usually winds up paying for the rent increases it allows. Most tenants are smart enough to figure that out. It's when bad management of the project starts taking its toll that problems can occur, of course.

From a pure real estate point of view, Section 8s can meet certain basic criteria in that they often provide decent housing to complement a neighborhood's demographics, and protect the landlord's interests. There's flexibility in that the housing can be designed for families or elderly couples, or a combination, in high-rise or garden-type apartments, in a suburban or inner-city location. These are definite pluses over some prior government projects which restricted tenant amenities and site selections.

From a tax point of view, there are all the attractions of accelerated depreciation, full and immediate deductions for interest, taxes, and carrying charges during the construction phase which are not available to other real estate projects under the provisions of the Tax Reform Act of 1976. In addition, the leverage on these deals —up to 85% of the project's cost—is exempt from the at-risk provisions of the Tax Reform Act of 1976 as well.

But you've got to be very careful about how the numbers work out, or the long arm of the IRS may come to tap you on the shoulder.

The problem is that some developers and syndicators are selling Section 8 deals at a premium. Let's say it costs $5 million to put up a Section 8 project, and HUD requires that the limited partners put up 15%—or $750,000—in equity. But the up-front deductions based on leverage are so good that investors might be willing to pay $1.5 million to get into the deal. The extra $750,000 could go right into the promoter's pocket in the form of lots of interesting fees and covenants if you're not careful. If this happens, the economics can get totally out of whack.

If the project is expected to generate a $50,000 cash flow each year, that's a 6.7% return on equity of $750,000. But on an investment of $1.5 million, the return is 3.3%. Lest you think that's no big deal, remember that most if not all of the cash flow in the early years of these deals is sheltered from taxes through depreciation and operating expenses.

Another problem to look out for is the depreciation schedule the promoter is attaching to the useful life of the project. Some promoters have been known to assign 10-year useful lives to projects the IRS later determines should be depreciated over 35 or 40 years. Remember, the investor will pay the difference after an audit, *not* the promoter.

"The problem with Section 8s is that many projects are simply not good investments," says Von R. Smith, president of Southwest Asset Management, Inc., a financial planning firm in Ft. Worth, Texas. In order for a deal to survive, you sometimes need 98% occupancy year-round, with people paying their share of the rent on time. "Unfortunately, many of the people who rent Section 8 apartments have no money to begin with. That's why the government takes care of them," notes a skeptical Merrill Lynch stockbroker who refuses to sell these deals to his clients.

Here are some useful tips on analyzing any particular deal:

• Check out the area in which the project is to be built. Is it growing or declining? If it's in decline, demand for apartments may fall off in the future. Moreover, the building may have no residual value at the end of 20 years or whenever the HUD contract expires. "I've never seen a government project which could be sold for its construction costs," notes Smith. "These projects rarely appreciate in value like real estate should." Of course, if the area you're looking into is growing, there may be a chance that you will be able to convert the building to some other use when its HUD life expires.

• Find out what the market is for low-income housing development in the area. If other Section 8s already exist, find out how they're doing. Visit the area yourself. Make sure you won't be walking into a deal where the supply of Section 8s in a given area is already too great for the market to absorb. And make sure that some other government project—like a development sponsored by HUD's Urban Development Action Grant Program (UDAG)—isn't already on the books, which could cause neighborhood dislocations and community conflicts.

• Determine whether the Section 8 housing is designed for the elderly or low-income families, says Smith. Generally speaking, buildings designed for the elderly are a safer bet than those designed for families, because they have more apartments, elevators, and a larger market to draw from. The senior citizen market, which is growing rapidly, is more dependable and stable than many other kinds of low-income groups. Cash management is less of a problem because the elderly generally pay their bills on time and skip out less often. Maintenance is usually less of a problem with elderly people, many of whom may be used to keeping their living quarters and surrounding areas clean and efficient. It all boils down to a question of management competence: Will the promoter be able to provide a safe, clean environment so that residents will be proud of their homes, or will the management be so slipshod that the tenants "take over," and enforce their demands with rent strikes?

• Consider the problem of recapture very carefully in any Section 8 deal. Recapture is the one tax bugaboo which some promoters are likely to ignore or pay some self-assuring lip service toward when selling a deal. It can provide a host of problems down the road, says Smith of Southwest Asset Management, even though real estate profits are taxed at lower capital gains rates, rather than ordinary income tax rates, if held longer than a year.

"When you get deductions up front which exceed your original investment, you wind up with a negative basis on which to compute your capital gain," notes Smith. And since you can't get out of a Section 8 syndicate until all the limited partners exit (through sale, or, alas, foreclosure), you may be stuck with some big tax bills down the road.

Recapture is an intricate process which subjects accelerated depreciation taken in excess of straight-line depreciation to *ordinary* income tax rates (up to 70% as opposed to 28% on capital gains) upon sale or disposition of property held less than a certain period of time. Hence, if you bought into a Section 8 syndicate for $50,000, and accelerated depreciation generated $100,000 in losses, you'd have a couple of tax problems. First, the minimum tax on preference items could subject the accelerated depreciation to 15% tax going into the deal.

Then let's say the deal is sold five years down the line. All the depreciation in excess of straight-line is considered part of your "gain" on the sale of the property.

Worse yet, notes Smith, if the deal goes belly-up, investors would be subject to recapture at ordinary rates which will not be based on the book value of the bankrupt property, but on the original mortgage held on the property. Hence if 20 investors put $50,000 each in a $5 million deal, the equity would be $1 million (20 × $50,000); the mortgage would be $4 million. The excess depreciation taken on the property in the first five years may amount to $20,000 more than the straight-line depreciation would have produced. If, after five years, the mortgage is foreclosed, each investor would stand to take a "gain" of $20,000 and pay taxes as high as $14,000 on that paper gain, depending on the taxpayer's bracket at the time of sale or foreclosure. In crueler terms, those up-front paper losses have generated back-end paper gains which might motivate investors to make paper dolls out of the deal's prospectus, and sausage out of the promoter.

"You've got a negative asset on which you will have to pay some tax at some point in a Section 8 deal," notes Von Smith, "unless the property is held for more than 100 months, in which case no recapture tax would be owed." A Section 8 deal is designed as a long-term investment, but it is fraught with pitfalls on the operations end which could trigger some very nasty short-term tax blows.

The savvy, well-heeled investor with large tax problems, a battery of highly paid advisors, and a keen eye for the real estate business can probably benefit from a well-structured Section 8 deal, or similar deals designed for the elderly under Section 515 of the Department of Agriculture's Farm Home Loan Bank program. The latter are beginning to crop up more frequently, and are

designed strictly for communities of less than 20,000
people, but there are not that many experienced promoters around with sound track records yet. There are
some organizations with good Section 8 track records,
and these might be considered worthy of inspection by
high-risk-taking heavy hitters.

But the conservative investor who's wooed with visions of big tax deductions and hefty cash flow scores on
Section 8 deals would be wise to sit down and read the
prospectus carefully. Then, one should talk to the syn-
dicator to discover all the red tape he had to go through
in order to get the project approved. Then one might
ask: "If this guy went to so much trouble to get this deal
off the ground, what's the reason he's coming to me for
equity? Is he too far along to bail out, and needs me to
bail him out? Or is he so generous that he's willing to
share his profits with me, a total stranger?" The answer
to that, and your belief in the availability of a free lunch,
may help determine if you're the breed of cat to go into a
Section 8, or whether you'd be better off turning on the
television on Saturday morning to catch the original ver-
sion of "Looney Tunes."

12.

Commercial Property, Or Investing Where America Works

Much of the action in real estate syndicates has shifted over the past several years into commercial properties— places where people work for a living—as opposed to previous emphasis on apartment complexes. That's because well-located, solidly leased office buildings and shopping centers offer some advantages which residential properties can't match, especially in light of what we've discussed in our previous two chapters.

There are, however, still some *caveats* to look out for when shopping for a commercial property deal, and most experts agree that it all boils down to a question of qualified management. Running an office building or a shopping center is a tricky business, since you're basically dealing with a whole bunch of entrepreneurs who have their own ideas on how to run a business (sometimes the landlord's). For this reason, the comments in this chapter come largely from conversations I've had over a number of years with a trio of respected and successful commercial property experts.

C. Everett Steichen is an old pro in the commercial property game, going back over three decades into the beginnings of urban renewal and shopping center development activities which began right after the end of World War II. Former president and chairman of Larry Smith & Company, an influential real estate consulting firm in its day, Everett now runs his own consulting firm out of Palo Alto, California. He numbers the National Retail Merchants Association as one of his prized clients, and is generally acknowledged as one of the leading shopping center development and management people around. I like him because he can look at a piece of undeveloped land and usually come up with a viable, tasteful use for it conceptually without too much fuss. He also has steadfastly worn white shirts and bow ties for all the years I've known him, which at least makes him consistent.

Samuel G. Friedman, Jr., chairman of AFCO Realty Associates in Atlanta, has turned the job of office building management into a near art form in that overly anxious city, with the result that he can size up location, design, and expense figures intuitively to tell whether or not you've got a good deal on your hands. He's also not greedy, a rare and stabilizing quality in a real estate entrepreneur from the Sunbelt. A prime mover behind San Antonio's massive downtown redevelopment project, Sam turns down more assignments than he cares to count in order to devote most of his time to matters he understands best. He also knows he looks terrible in bow ties.

Richard Wollack retired in his mid-thirties from First Capital Companies, a commercial property investment/management firm he co-founded in Coral Gables, Florida. Now perched at the top of one of the hills surrounding San Francisco as a guru to other real estate syndicators, Dick is affiliated with Consolidated Capital

Institutional Advisors in Emeryville, operating in a manner which befits a Stanford MBA: sound philosophic outlook and a nasty eye for money.

"Office buildings are a better hedge on the downside than apartments," says Wollack. He notes that office buildings enjoy greater stability, longer leases, predictable market structures, low vacancy rates, and more specialized management expertise. What's more, a business must still operate from a central location and pay its rent—even in bad times. By contrast, apartment dwellers can pack up and move in with friends and relatives. On the other hand, the advantages of office building ownership in sour economic times can work against you in boom times, he notes. Rents usually can't be raised quickly to keep up with market demand if a building has a majority of tenants with long-term, fixed leases, he says. Such are the variables of life.

While the market variables of an office building are sometimes easier to predict than those of residential properties, these experts stress the "sometimes." The rules of analyzing any tax shelter deal also apply to a potential investment in a syndicate which proposes to buy or build commercial properties, says Wollack.

While most commercial experts are reluctant to assign arbitrary rate-of-return projections to commercial properties, there are some "comfort guidelines" which you can apply, notes Sam Friedman. "If the leases are with strong national or regional companies, or on a net-net-net basis—where the tenants pay most of the maintenance costs—I'd be happy with a rate-of-return that gave me 1% or 2% more than I could get in a bank savings account," he states. "In a riskier situation, where there's no large anchor tenant such as a department store or a major corporation, I'd try to shoot for a higher return."

Getting a handle on rate-of-return for commercial deals is complicated by some new rules of real estate investments. Institutional investors and foreign buyers have been gobbling up commercial real estate in a big way over the past few years. While institutions such as REITs, insurers, and pension funds drive a harder bargain than foreign investors, foreigners are more interested in safety and liquidity than in high yield, says Wollack. Moreover, they tend to pay pretty close to top dollar to get what they want. And foreign investors even seem willing to forsake a good yield just to gain a stake in this country—often paying cash for property which can be easily financed. "They feel that the United States is the safest place in the world to invest," notes Everett Steichen, "or, at least, our real estate is safe, when compared to the rising inflation and increased terrorism in other parts of the world."

Europeans, especially, feel this way, adds Sam Friedman. "They remember that during the Great Depression the one commodity which did not lose value was well-located real estate." For foreigners, the watershed was Watergate; when they saw that the United States did not go down the tubes after a president resigned in disgrace, they went bananas and began shoveling *deutsche marks, francs, yen, lire,* and some of our own dollars into the coffers of lucky real estate owners here.

However, there's a second-tier of prime properties which offer individuals very attractive investment opportunities at good prices and handsome yields which are not the prime targets of big overseas bucks, says Dick Wollack. He defines second-tier as properties in strong markets, available for $5 million or less, and managed by promoters who are intimately familiar with the market these properties are in. These are deals the big boys overlook.

One other point: The axiom of investing close to home can be stretched somewhat in the case of commercial property—if you're familiar with the market and confident of management, says Wollack. Even so, remember that a promoter with buildings all over the place is still at a distinct disadvantage, management-wise, compared to a promoter who sticks to one city or state.

"Look at a deal from a total economic point of view," says Wollack. Assess the strength of the market. If there's just a 5% to 7% office building vacancy rate in the market, chances are the area's not overbuilt. Reason: Overall vacancies include second or third-rate properties which may have more empty space—and that tends to mask a shortage of prime space. Shopping centers, however, are another matter altogether. "There isn't a major market in the country which isn't close to being over-built right now, or restricted by environmental laws," says Everett Steichen. He notes, however, that the secondary markets—cities with population in the 150,000 to 300,000 range—may be in for a boom shortly, for major retailers are looking in these locations for expansion.

Check out the prevailing rental rates in the market. If a property you're looking at is getting absolutely top rental rates, there's a risk that a competitor could build a new structure close by and cut your market by charging either the same, or less. Hence, you'd be wise to find out what a developer would have to pay—and charge—to compete with you, and still stay afloat, says Wollack. If your building is getting a healthy cash flow and good return at rental rates which are below the top-of-the-market, you may have a good deal—especially if leases will turn over within a few years.

Look at the tenancy structure. If the market is geared to one or two industries, you should try to get a fix on what would happen to your vacancy rate should those businesses run into bad times. In the case of small, strip shopping centers, location, tenant mix, and life-styles also play a prime role. A shopping center with a boutique makeup must depend on an affluent, trendy market, or a stable tourist center. That's especially true if it doesn't have a supermarket or major national retailer to act as an anchor tenant, says Steichen.

If a promoter is offering a sale-leaseback deal involving a property which the promoter already manages for a tenant/owner or a financial institution, there are some key questions to ask. Why is the seller trying to unload the property? If it's that good, why not keep it and reap the cash flow and tax benefits? There are generally only three good reasons which should interest you:

First, "a retailer may have to raise cash for inventory expansion or to open other branches," says Steichen. Second, he says, "he simply may not want to be involved in managing real estate any more." The same holds true for banks and insurers, even though many of them have created large real estate investment departments recently. They'll invest, but don't want to manage—like limited partners on a large scale. Third, a publicly owned company, while enjoying the tax benefits of depreciation, may want to improve its bottom line to impress Wall Street analysts, adds Richard Wollack. "The company may need earnings-per-share rather than cash flow or yield to impress the skeptics on the Street," he says. Wall Street can sometimes be confused when it sees a company flush with rental income, but reduced earnings, resulting from a reduction in its tax base through real estate accounting methods. This may present a good opportunity to investors seeking some tax shelter and good cash flow.

If the promoter already manages some properties, talk to some of the current tenants. You'll get a pretty good handle on his ability as a manager by chatting about cleanliness, maintenance services, such as heating and air conditioning, security, etc. The property should be managed by the promoter or an affiliate to keep cost-control incentives within the confines of the partnership; or by a reputable local firm that's not spread out all over the country. This is crucial, says Wollack: A well-managed building is a boon to the tenants' business— hence, to the owners.

Management fees between 3% and 5% of gross receipts are reasonable, says Sam Friedman. As for incentives or bonuses, he sums it up by saying that the major incentive to the promoter/manager is "to go after the prime prospects, sign sound leases, fill up the building, give good service, and control costs so that he can increase his management fee by improving the cash flow and rate-of-return for the owners."

Basically, that's what you're looking for in any tax shelter.

Part Four

Energy—Oil On Troubled Wallets, Coal In Your Socks

13.

You Don't Need A Consciousness Group To Generate Positive Energy

You could stand back and take a look at all the terrible things which have been done by the Internal Revenue Service to tax shelter deals in oil and gas and coal mining over the past 10 years and come to the conclusion that these guys don't know there's an energy crisis going on. After all, if the nation needs all the fossilized fuel it can get its wasteful hands on, then the least the IRS can do is make some positive moves toward encouraging investors to take risks, rather than virtually putting the freeze on some of these deals.

The same can be said for Congress and the past few administrations. It seems that every time we're told by either branch of the government that we've got to find more domestic sources of energy, Congress eliminates the oil depletion allowance, or the executive branch presses for a windfall profits tax. My father has an expression for this kind of situation: *"Managgia l'America!"* Casey Stengel translated it as *"Can't Anyone Here Play This Game?"*

If you look deeper, however, into the reasons why various kinds of deals in energy tax shelters have been given the old squeezo recently, you may come up with a different perspective on the question at hand. Now, I'm not one to give the IRS a standing ovation on any occasion (polite applause is about all you'll get from me), but the fact of the matter is that when they took corrective action against coal shelters, and tightened up scrutiny of oil and gas deals during the 1970s, the folks at the Service may have done high-bracket investors more good than harm. That's because some of the most outrageous abuses in the tax shelter world have occurred in oil and gas drilling and coal mining deals.

Now, with energy once again a hot topic, the word is out that after a couple of years of relative calm, some fairly unscrupulous promoters are on the prowl again, looking for suckers to fleece, ready with a slap on the back and a ready smile, bellowing out in their best wildcatter's drawl or miner's clip, "I'm gonna make you a million dollars, boy!" Who cares who shot J.R. on "Dallas"? *These* are the guys who are dangerous.

The attraction in energy, of course, is the price. All it took was a few ballsy Arabs to make petroleum a viable investment again, tax considerations aside. And the price of coal, while certainly not skyrocketing, has moved up a bit since the early 1970s; and we all know how many articles have been written about the need to double, triple, or even quintuple our use of coal over the next couple of decades—that's bound to affect prices, right?

Right. Except . . .

It's not that easy to find oil or gas and, in many cases, when it's found, it's awfully expensive to get it out of the ground. Secondly, nobody seems to be buying much coal these days, and if you can't sell it, "why make it?" Add to this the scandals which occasionally crop up in this whole business of energy, and you've got a tax shelter opportunity, yes, but one to be especially careful in evaluating in the early 1980s.

Oil and gas tax shelters are offered on both a public and private basis, and while it is certainly true that most of the tax and economic abuses in tax shelters *per se* come in those deals offered privately, you run just as high a risk of blowing the jewels, so to speak, in a public oil/gas deal than in one offered to a select few. The growth of oil/gas tax shelters has been nothing short of phenomenal over the past few years. In 1979 alone, investors pumped a record-breaking $1.05 billion into public drilling ventures, according to Resource Programs, Inc., a New York City firm which provides all sorts of interesting information as the data source of the business. The previous year, $670 million was raised for these public ventures. While that's a lot of dough, it may pale by comparison to the amount raised for private drilling activities and, in most cases, we are talking in both public and private deals of ventures which will drill domestically. Most of the foreign stuff is still handled by the Texacos and Mobils, which one would suspect are not that short of funds for drilling purposes.

Oil and gas tax shelters are the province of the "independent" oil companies. These are generally either one-man shops put together by some disgruntled, and possibly brilliant, geologist, or publicly held exploration firms which are in the business of finding oil and gas, not refining or selling it to the public. Thus, there's a mind-boggling range of company sizes, locations, philosophies, and competence to consider when scrutinizing any opportunity in this tax shelter. Sometimes, to make matters more complicated, an oil company with five employees can be far more successful in locating oil or gas for investors than a public company with $100 million in revenues. It doesn't always happen that way, but it's not an uncommon phenomenon in the business. As is true in any tax shelter, you can generally gauge the seriousness of the promoter/driller by the amount of money which will be siphoned off the front-end of investors' contributions in the form of fees to management. If less than 85% of your money is to be spent on drilling wells, chances are the promoter is quite content to live off the remaining 20% or more; and if he finds oil with your money, well, it's a nice bonus.

Coal, on the other hand, is a relatively new tax shelter, and one which has had a roller coaster, sorry history. When movie tax shelters were censored by the IRS, promoters of these deals moved into coal. These are the kinds of people who like to keep things out of the eye of the IRS and SEC, so you'll rarely find a public coal deal, notes Bill Brennan, publisher of the newsletter, *Brennan Reports*. That's because they're packagers, not operators or managers. They go where the action is at the moment. "I'd say that 90% of the promoters who first went into coal in 1976 were previously packaging movie deals," he says. "Then when the going in coal got rough, they switched into master recordings and books. When the IRS issued adverse rulings on recordings, they started coming back to coal."

There are still tax and investment advantages in some coal deals for someone with a minimum of $25,000 to invest, Brennan advises. But he cautions that if you're looking into energy, and you're working with less cash than $25,000, and are worried about the risk of an IRS audit, you'd be better off in oil and gas. Coming from a "coal man," that's pretty objective advice, I'd say.

By contrast, the promoter of an oil and gas shelter usually acts as the General Partner and, in the case of public deals, most have been offering programs for quite a while. There's been an enormous shakeout in the number of oil/gas promoters since the early 1970s, or at least those who offer public deals. Some of the shadier characters have cropped up of late with private offerings, and they're the ones to look out for.

The main difference between oil and gas and coal shelters can be seen in promoter attitudes and investor motivations. Coal promoters usually lure new investors into the tax shelter with a promise of high up-front write-offs. In the old days (say, 1977), these used to run as high as 5 to 1. By paying mineral royalties in advance (a practice effectively squashed by the IRS since then), an investor could deduct them right away. So, a $25,000 investment could generate a $125,000 tax deduction the first year. Today, the write-offs are far less, but the deals are still sold on a tax-shelter-first, economic-reward-second, basis.

There are hopes that coal leasing promoters may follow the lead of oil and gas promoters—who were forced into emphasizing economics (and not tax shelter) when the IRS cracked down on tax abuses which occurred during the go-go years of 1969-73. Those tax-wise, but investment-foolish, drilling deals based on high leverage led directly to the at-risk provisions of the Tax Reform Act of 1976.

So, coal deals, if they become popular based on the price of the product resulting from a sudden demand, may go the way of oil and gas: tax shelter will take a back seat to economic viability. And that's not all bad. At least an investor will be a little more certain about getting something for his or her hard-earned cash.

It's gotten to the point in oil and gas where an investor can realistically expect no more than a 90% up-front write-off. Consequently, the smart investors now ask: "How much cash flow and total return can I expect on my investment, tax considerations aside?" That's the new tax shelter question everyone should ask.

14.

A Brief Look At Coal: Patience May Keep You Out Of The Pits

Even though most coal deals have been the pits for unwary investors, there are some which might offer a chance at mining some reasonable tax as well as investment benefits. What it takes is patience, diligence, and a minimum of $25,000 to invest.

Patience you need because demand for coal must rise far higher for the price to become economically viable. Diligence will require an expenditure of some cash *before* selecting any deal (tax-deductible anyway). And the $25,000 minimum comes in because coal deals are private, and require a heftier ticket to get in.

Toward the end of the 1970s, coal shelters started to make economic, as well as tax, sense. That's because the repeated attacks on coal shelters by the IRS and the SEC forced the promoters of these deals into cleaning up their act, says Bill Brennan, who acted as a consultant to coal companies for many years prior to publishing *Brennan Reports*. This chapter is based on various chats with him.

Here's how the poorly structured coal deals used to work and, if rumors are to be believed, some of these may still be around.

A promoter acquires the rights to mine coal from a landowner by offering a royalty based on a fixed price per ton. The promoter then wheels and deals the rights to investors who pay, say, $25,000 each to get into the deal. The problem is that the investor's ante is eaten up by the promoter's fee and the advance royalty due the owner of the land. So, the promoter then takes a note back from the investors, say, $100,000, to cover as many as 20 years' worth of future royalties. The $100,000 note, which is secured by the coal in the ground—if any—is then paid off through the investor's share of the proceeds from the coal. The investor then deducts the $25,000 he put into the deal as well as the $100,000 note he put up in the year the investment is made.

The trouble is, the IRS has attacked the advance royalty scheme. Some promoters and attorneys feel they can still fight this IRS position because they interpret Congress's intent of the tax laws far differently than the IRS. The prevailing view, however, is that if any advance royalties are to be taken, it should be for only one year, similar to a real estate situation wherein rent paid in advance from December of one year through November of the next has been held to be perfectly legal.

Another problem with this kind of scheme, of course, is that the investor is at-risk for the $100,000 note. What happens if there is, indeed, no coal under the land? Or, it's of the wrong quality and not marketable? This brings up another problem with deals structured in this manner. Many promoters quote unrealistic coal prices to make the deal attractive to investors. The coal is actually mined by a contractor who used his own money to bring in men and equipment to extract the coal. The mining contractor's payoff is a set dollar per ton mined. For example, this is the way the payout may work in one of these deals:

The promoter says the coal is worth $25 a ton, of which the contractor will take $16 to cover his costs. That leaves the investor with a gross return of $9 a ton. While that seems like a nice margin on the surface, almost half of it will probably be siphoned off by the promoter to pay off the $100,000 notes. That still leaves $4 or $5 a ton for the investor. That's OK—except for two variables: the contractor still gets $16 a ton, no matter what. If coal is selling at $20 in the market, the margin is significantly narrower. Then, there just might not be that much coal in that mine—even though the investor's on the hook for the advanced royalties.

By contrast, the new type of coal shelter will offer investors a good tax advantage and a decent chance to make a return on their investments, says Brennan. First, the advance royalty would be paid for one year, as noted above. Then, part of the money will be used to acquire the mining contractor's equipment. This will generate an immediate investment tax credit as well as interest and depreciation deductions.

The maximum first-year write-off in a deal like this will be no more than 150% or so, and may be a lot less, notes Brennan. But that's about all one can reasonably expect in any kind of economically viable tax shelter these days.

There are five key areas to check out when considering a coal promoter, says Brennan. It may cost you some money, but it's well worth the risk considering the money you may be investing. Besides, it's deductible if you go into the deal.

(1) Find out what kind of experience the promoter has in coal. Chances are, you'll find that 90% of the promoters now in coal were in some other kind of "exotic" tax shelter business before. Avoid them. You want someone who's totally familiar with the way the coal industry works. So check out bank references, previous employment experience, and even the experience of his law and accounting firms. If he operates out of some beach in Florida, how much does he really know about the hills and holes of Pennsylvania?

(2) Check out the promoter's mining contractor. Find out how much experience the contractor has and if he has the equipment needed to do the job. Also find out if he plans to use union or non-union labor. Non-union labor may not be allowed to mine the area where you've invested. Check the contractor's reputation with banks and mining companies in the area.

(3) Make sure that mining permits for the land you're leasing are available. If someone is now farming on top of a coal lode, he may not care if you're stuck with lease rights, and there are state, local, or federal restrictions to mining that coal now. After all, he has your advance royalties already. So, find out who really owns the land, talk to them personally, and get some unassailable third-party opinions.

(4) Ask for an independent geologist's report on the quality of the coal and the estimated reserves. There are

many types of coal—anthracite, steam, metallurgical, low-medium-and-high-volatile coal. Each grade has its own market and price. If an independent geologist's report isn't available, you can commission one for around $1,000 or so. While that's not cheap, it could be the key factor in your overall evaluation of the deal.

(5) Make sure the sales price for coal that the promoter is quoting jibes with reality. Spot coal prices are published each week by *Coal Week,* and give the indication of the price you can expect to get for your lode. A sample copy of *Coal Week* may be obtained from McGraw-Hill's Newsletter Center, 1221 Avenue of the Americas, New York, New York 10020.

Following this advice might not bring you tremendous wealth, but it may assure you coal in your Christmas stocking, at the very least.

15.

A Taxing Look At
Oil And Gas Ventures

Perhaps no other investment has been more debated, denounced, glorified, promoted, analyzed, reformed, and misunderstood than oil and gas drilling funds. (Yes, real estate included; but real estate is hardly always an investment—it's a way of life.) Since 1968, when they first became standard conversational hors d'oeuvres—or bromides—at chic cocktail parties, drilling funds have become the most popular tax shelter around, with, again, the possible exception of real estate. Yet despite the chatter, instead of being one of the easiest tax shelters to understand, oil and gas ventures have become one of the most difficult to evaluate.

The reasons are complex. Drilling for oil and gas, by its very nature, often seems to be a mixture of ancient alchemy and modern geology. For every well drilled and abandoned in the Baltimore Canyon, it seems that all someone has to do in Ohio is stick a finger into the ground and gas fizzes up. (It is rumored that so much gas has come up out of Ohio that the state is floating on a layer of air where the gas used to be, and is poised to sink below Indiana, Pennsylvania, and Kentucky like some giant cutout on a map.)

To make matters worse, Congress, various administrations, and the IRS have turned the tax aspects of
these ventures into a myriad of codes and rules—which
often seem to be in direct conflict with our national
energy policies (assuming we have any). The accounting
methods involved often approach the Byzantine, to say
nothing of the bizarre. To top it off, some oil operators
still prey on the pipe dreams of unsophisticated investors—successfully, more often than not.

Investors still make the mistake of going into oil and
gas drilling funds for tax reasons only, according to
most financial advisors I've talked to recently. However,
"Congress has watered down the tax incentives of drilling so much that we don't even consider it a tax shelter
any more," says Terry Gill, a financial planner with Professionals' Financial Group, Fort Worth. In reality, he
says, these ventures are now either a capital gains play,
tax deferral maneuver, or a hedge against inflation.

Moreover, it's an investment you should be prepared
to live with, and feed, for some time, says James D.
Schwartz, who heads his own financial planning firm in
Denver, the new energy capital of the West. You
shouldn't even consider a drilling venture unless you're
prepared to stick with drilling as an investment strategy
for at least three years. What's more, Schwartz advises
that you'd also be wise to invest in a diversified portfolio
of drilling funds to spread your risk. The things that can
go wrong with any one of these funds can add up to more
horrors than were crammed into Pandora's Box.
Schwartz's diversified approach will be explained further in the next chapter.

How much you get to deduct in a drilling fund
depends on how the money you've invested is spent. Up-
front write-offs are allowed for "intangible drilling
costs" only. According to the Tax Code, these are expen-

ditures for wages, fuel, repairs, hauling, supplies, and
other items needed to drill wells and prepare them for
production. In a typical deal, the intangibles amount to
only 70% or 90% of the investor's total contribution.

As for tax sheltering income from producing wells,
the oil depletion allowance, which excluded a portion of
revenues from any taxes, is gradually being phased out.
The windfall profits tax, while affecting those people
who invest with independent drillers, should not have
any effect, or a minimal one, on most investors, says
Robert Stanger, publisher of *The Stanger Report*. That's
because up to 1,000 barrels of oil per day production is
excluded from the tax if it comes out of a well drilled by
an independent. (There is no windfall tax on gas.) This
1,000 barrel limit applies to each partner in a limited
partnership, so you'd have to discover a new North
Slope before you worry about the effects of the tax. And
if you've got the North Slope, you can start your own
country and chuck the tax.

In a well-structured deal, about 85% of your money
should be used for intangibles, says Jim Schwartz.
"Anybody who tells you that you can still get a 200%
write-off in oil and gas is selling you a gimmick," he
says. And it's just not worth the risk. The gimmick these
days is the "letter of credit" deal, and here's how it
works.

The promoter skirts the at-risk rules for a tax shelter
by telling an investor that he or she can leverage deductions higher by issuing a letter of credit. I had a long conversation with my old friend David Gracer about this a
short while before his untimely passing, and he summed
up the letter of credit ploy with these words: "This is a
potential time bomb which can have the effect of con-
tributing to scandals in this industry the likes of which
you haven't seen since Black Watch Farm and Home-

stake Petroleum." Those deals were famous for the chic personalities who were attracted to, and defrauded by, shoddy deals in cattle raising and oil drilling.

A letter of credit that's issued by an investor is secured by his or her other assets, such as the investor's home, stocks, and bonds. The promoter uses the letter of credit to borrow from a bank. The bank has no risk. It will be paid out of the oil and gas revenues—or the investor's hide. The promoter isn't taking a risk either. As a matter of fact, he may even boost his management fee by basing it on the original investment as well as on the borrowed funds. You guessed it: The investor gets stuck with all the risks.

There are two other major dangers in this kind of arrangement. One, the IRS may eventually question the validity of this kind of deal, which, *ex post facto,* could destroy all your nicely leveraged tax deductions. Two, some promoters who use gimmicks like this have a notorious reputation for drilling dry holes. If that happens, the assets used to back up the note will be in jeopardy.

You are personally liable to pay off that letter of credit. There is no guarantee, even if you find oil or gas at the bottom of the hole, that the revenues will be enough to cover your original investment, plus the letter of credit. Don't be greedy in oil and gas; it's one of the reasons J.R. got his comeuppance on "Dallas," remember.

Even a 70% to 90% write-off in a valid oil and gas deal will come to less than you might have expected in tax deductions—thanks to the 15% minimum tax on preference items, notes Bill Brennan. While this tax affects some other tax shelters as well, it comes down particularly hard on oil and gas ventures. Reason: Write-offs for intangible drilling costs are considered a "preference item." In real estate, for example, only accelerated depreciation is treated that way; up-front interest deductions and straight-line depreciation are not subject to the minimum tax.

And there's very little you can do to escape the minimum tax, says Brennan. You can only reduce the liability by using a $10,000 statutory allowance or base the tax on one-half your total income tax liability, whichever is greater, he notes.

Here's how the numbers work out. Assume you invest $50,000 in a drilling deal which produced a $35,000 (70%) first-year write-off. Also assume that your income tax liability is $22,000 after taking that $35,000 deduction. You're going to wind up paying $25,600 in taxes, not $22,000, as you might expect. The numbers, please:

A. Tax preference item	$35,000
B. (Less) ½ of income tax, or	
$10,000, whichever is higher	(11,000)
C. Amount subject to tax	24,000
D. 15% minimum tax on $24,000	3,600
E. Income tax liability	22,000
F. Total tax liability (D + E)	$25,600

There's yet another wonderful complication, says Brennan. The minimum tax triggers a process which may actually subject you to a higher tax rate than the 50% ceiling on earned income. When you invest in oil and gas, you may, in effect, remove a portion of your income from the favorable 50% rate and subject it to a rate of up to 70%. As a result, the rule of thumb which says if you're in the 50% bracket and invest $50,000 in a 100% deductible venture (for argument's and simplicity sake), you'll cut your taxes by $25,000 ain't necessarily so. Once again, the digits:

	Without Investment*	With Investment*
Gross income	$160,000	$160,000
Deductions & exemptions	(10,000)	(10,000)
(Loss)—investment in 100% deductible oil deal	-0-	(50,000)
Taxable income	150,000	100,000
Ordinary tax	62,449	37,499
PLUS minimum tax	-0-	4,688
Total tax	$ 62,449	$ 42,187

Married, filing jointly.

The actual tax savings is only $20,312, not the $25,000 you expected. So, your 100% deductible investment actually turns out to be an 80% deduction, because the $20,312 bottom line tax savings is only 40% of $50,000. So much for *caveat emptor de taxibus.*

You damn well better find *something* down at the bottom of that hole.

16.

Of Wildcatters, Dentists, And Other Drillers ...

To be absolutely blunt about it, oil and gas deals are incredibly hard to evaluate. Sure, finding a well-structured deal that's run by a promoter with a sterling track record will improve your odds of making some petrodollars. And, at today's prices of up to $40 a barrel for newly discovered oil (as opposed to around four bucks back in the early 1970s), a couple of good wells in a small program can produce a bonanza.

But you're just as likely to have as much success putting your money on a dentist who's drilling the cavities of a well-heeled sheik: There may be oil down there in the gums, you know!

To be serious, however, when all is said and done, despite all the seismological, computerized advances of modern petroleum technology, drilling is still pretty much of a crapshoot. When I worked in public relations, one of my clients, The Ballard & Cordell Corporation of Atlanta, a drilling program promoter, would always caution me to be very careful about reporting the successful wells they'd discovered. Once, when a particularly large discovery was made in Louisiana, you could hear the cheers from the company's small staff echoing through the canyons of Peachtree Street as the reports came in from the field office. "Don't get too excited, boy," cautioned Perry Ballard, the president of the company. "We still have to get that stuff *out* of the ground." Indeed, as it turned out, it took a good deal more money, and many months' effort, before that well began to generate the revenue everyone had expected. So many things can go wrong.

In fact, most financial advisors think that oil and gas shelters are so risky that only the financially secure should even consider the gamble. According to our friend Jim Schwartz of Denver, you shouldn't even think of an oil and gas deal unless you have the staying power to invest $5,000 to $10,000 each year for three consecutive years in a diversified portfolio of exploratory, development, and balanced programs, preferably with the same promoter. And then invest in the beginning of the year, when the best deals are available, and try to do so with a publicly owned company whose stock is traded on a recognized exchange. Why? "They have to find oil, or the price of their stock won't go up," he says. "As a hedge," he continues, "I'd also buy stock in the company."

Some definitions are in order here about the kinds of wells which are drilled, and the types of drilling programs available:

• *Exploratory wells*—also known as wildcats—are drilled in search of new pools of oil or gas or drilled in the hopes of greatly expanding the limits of an existing pool of dinosaur remains. Five out of six exploratory wells come up dry, on average, which means you sinks your money in and wave bye-bye with crossed fingers, toes— and possibly, eyes. If you hit, it's usually a bonanza.

• *Development wells* are like going to the dentist. They are drilled in previously discovered oil fields to exploit an already known producing formation. A very good development program could hit 75% of the wells drilled. But like a dentist, the driller knows where the cavity is—he just has to hit it right on the head to be successful. Even then, the revenues from development wells can be far less than exploratory wells in the same field, since you're drawing from the same source. Drilling for gas in Ohio and West Virginia is usually a development activity. You almost always get a rush of fizz with every hole you drill—but you can run into the old Belch Syndrome: once the gas escapes, the acid indigestion calms down, and sometimes the well doesn't pay for itself. Besides, Ohio's sinking.

• A *balanced program* is a package of exploratory and development drilling. Promoters figure that the development drilling will hedge against the probable losses in exploratory wells.

• A *completion program* should be avoided at all costs. This is a fairly new wrinkle where one limited partnership is formed to pay the "completion" costs of the wells drilled by another partnership. Completion of a well means getting it into production; as Perry Ballard said, finding oil or gas isn't enough—you've got to get it out. Sometimes, a promoter will hit several promising wells, but if he owned them himself, would probably not complete them because of the high costs involved and the probable marginal return on investment suggested.

However, if these wells belong to a limited partnership which has paid high up-front management fees to him, he may be willing to take the risk of completing the wells —with the money of a new partnership. In that case, the new partnership gets fewer up-front tax deductions (most of the intangible expenses accrue to the original partnership), and the revenue they are to receive from the wells is subordinated to the receipts of the original partners, and the banks which may have financed some of that partnership's activities. I find completion programs rife with fraud possibilities, although there may be one or two deals in the works at press time which could offer a more equitable sharing arrangement. One I've heard of would combine both drilling and completion activities in one partnership with two classes of limited partners, respectively. The folks who are toying with this concept are very bright and unusually adept at making money for their investors; if their concept works out, you'll read about it in the trade newsletters I've mentioned previously.

If you've never invested in oil or gas before, the experts suggest you look at public deals rather than private affairs. For one thing, drilling is very expensive, and with less than 35 investors in a private deal, the price of admission is usually very high. For another, since private deals don't have to pass SEC scrutiny on disclosures of prior activities, a promoter has the option of remaining silent about selected periods of his history. In fact, some promoters who've been indicted on securities fraud charges in some states, and are under SEC investigation, still trot around the country offering private deals, notes Terry Gill of Fort Worth. Even when these horrors are disclosed in a prospectus, people still invest. Reason: As ridiculous as it sounds, they haven't taken time to read the prospectus, says Gill.

Even though plowing through a prospectus is usually as exciting as rummaging through the *Congressional*

Record, you'll be able to spot some things that can make or break an oil deal. Jim Schwartz boils them down to *People, Structure, Liquidity, Assessments,* and *Performance.*

People: If the promoter of the deal is also the General Partner (and in oil and gas, the two can be separate), check out his track record. Find out how long he's been in the business and how his previous deals, if any, fared. If he hasn't been successful, perhaps it isn't all bad luck. Major oil companies have also been known to be incompetent when it comes to finding new oil.

If the deal is sponsored by a brokerage firm, find out who the operator or joint venturer will be. Also check out who will drill the wells—they're the ones to investigate, not the General Partner. If you can visit these people and look them in the eye as any smart business person would, you'll be able to size them up pretty fast.

Then check out the partnership's geologists. They're the ones charged with locating potential pools of hydrocarbons, as petroleum under the ground is called in the trade. A rapid turnover in the geological staff is a sure tip-off of problems, says Jim Schwartz. Geologists who find oil should be paid on an incentive basis to stick with the company; the competition for the good ones is too intense today for them to be on straight salary. Those who don't find oil and are still on the payroll should tell you something about the management's past performance.

Structure: The General Partner's financial commitment to the deal—mutuality of interest—has become an important criterion. Here's what we mean. In the past, the intangible drilling costs have been borne solely by the limited partners who could deduct them. The General Partner usually contributed the money needed to acquire leases and complete wells if hydrocarbons were encountered. However, if the well looked like it was

going to be only marginally profitable, the General Partner could save a lot of his money by abandoning it.
Presto. Nice write-off, no oil.

Some good promoters are now committing themselves to paying part of the intangible costs. While that
reduces the tax write-offs for the limited partners, it
gives the General Partner an added incentive to do all he
can to get the oil out of the ground. After all, his money
will go down the hole, too, if the well isn't commercially
viable.

You can tell if the General Partner is really your
partner if (1) he buys units in the partnership up front
and (2) his management fee does not exceed 4% or 5% of
what the limited partners put up. If he charges a higher
fee, it means less of your money will be used for drilling
and the promoter may be more interested in side trips to
Las Vegas than in drilling in Wyoming.

Sharing arrangements are important. You'd be wise
to choose a deal where the payout is based on the total
capital raised to drill all the partnership's wells. Here's
why: The limited partners generally get the lion's share
(up to 99%) of revenues from wells until payout—when
revenues start to exceed drilling and production costs.
Then the General Partner comes in for as much as 50%
of the profits. So, if you're in a program which has raised
$1 million and drilled 20 wells, and only one well (costing
$100,000) comes in commercial, only 10% of your money
will have to be returned before the General Partner
comes in for his bigger cut. This is known as *payout on a
well-to-well basis.* But if the arrangement is based on the
total partnership contributions ($1 million), you and the
other limited partners must get back $1 million before
the General Partner comes in for any substantial cut.
That's *payout on a program basis.*

As a concession to get the revenue sharing till payout arrangement on a program basis, the General Partner may ask for a higher percentage of revenue prior to payout (maybe 15% instead of 1%, you generous person, you). That's reasonable if he's committed some intangible drilling costs to the partnership.

Liquidity: Many programs will let you cash in your investment after a period of time—usually three years—which makes oil and gas drilling the most liquid of the illiquid tax shelters. Be very cautious about this—you could cheat yourself out of some nice income and place yourself in a tax trap, says Schwartz. Here's why:

The General Partner usually offers to liquidate your investment based on the *future net worth of proven reserves* in the ground. Generally, the future net worth is first discounted by a set percentage, which usually works out to 1% to 2% above the prime rate in effect at banks at the time. (The General Partner may have to borrow to finance his purchase.) Then, another 30% is usually lopped off to make up for any risk the General Partner will be left with. To make matters worse, the promoter will usually be very conservative in estimating the future value of *proven* reserves. Moreover, that's only proven reserves—not *probable* or *possible.* (All reserves are divided into three parts.) Hence, this formula could leave you with a net return of less than 30% of the future net worth of *all* reserves.

Even in a deal where that will give you $12,000 for each $10,000 you invested, you may be cutting off your nose to spite your face, says Schwartz. Reason: *There's more oil down there—and the price is rising.*

If that's not bad enough, get this: When you get out of an oil deal early, the intangible drilling costs that you deducted earlier may be recaptured—which could lead to a tax disability.

Assessments: In some programs, you may have to kick in some additional money, if the General Partner needs more to complete successful wells or drill development wells after finding a new field. In some cases, limited partners may have to ante up another 25% or more of their original investment. If the assessment is used for intangibles, you'll be able to squeeze some extra tax shelter from the deal. If it's used for capital costs, it will have to be amortized over a number of years—giving you a significantly lower tax break.

Assessments are either mandatory or optional. Both, if not paid, can result in substantial penalties to the investor. The way it usually works is that an investor who does not come up with the assessment loses his right to participate in revenues from the assessed activity until the General Partner—or whoever picked up the assessment, like a bank—has been repaid up to 300% of the assessment. Hence, the critical psychological element in oil and gas—staying power—becomes far more important where assessments are possible. Not only do you have to possess the cash flow to plan for future oil/gas investments, but also you have to have some loose change lying around to protect your current investment. "Always be ready to pay the assessment," says Schwartz, "especially in times of high interest rates." One, an assessment—especially in a program where there's mutuality of interest—usually means there's more oil down there. Two, if your interest becomes subordinated to a bank's high interest rate, you may never get "out of the hole."

Past Performance: "It's almost impossible to determine accurately whether an operator's past performance has resulted in good investments," says Schwartz. That's because of the way the tables in the "Prior Activities" sections of a typical prospectus are compiled.

The Limited Partners Payout Table usually lists the aggregate cash distributions—not the cash returned per investment unit. This can be further complicated by reserves reports—proven, possible, probable.

This is the point where you should ask for Investor Reports of previous partnerships, says Schwartz. Those write-ups will generally give you a clue as to whether or not the operator had a tough time working the wells to the point of commercial viability. "The longer and more frequent the reports on a partnership's activities, the greater the chances the General Partner has a history of problems," says Schwartz. When your well comes in, the greatest Investor Report you can receive in the future is a regular quarterly check.

Another performance indicator to look for in the prospectus is the liquidation ratios of prior partnerships. If the heavily discounted liquidation rate works out to 30 cents on the dollar, and the investor still made money, that might be a good operator. If the operator has a history of liquidating for far less than an even-up exchange even after being overly generous in the discounting arrangement, he might not be that adept at finding oil. You'd be better off sticking your finger in the ground somewhere around Steubenville or Akron.

Part Five

Farming—Tiptoe Through The Meadow Muffins

17.

How You Gonna Keep Them __Off__ The Farm After They've Seen Depreciation . . .

If you're one of those city slickers who's just about had it with steaming sidewalks and gleaming towers, hordes of commuters, and rising prices for food at the all-night supermarket, you've no doubt harbored escapist thoughts of chucking it all and heading out to the country to become a Gentleman Farmer. It all seems so easy, you think: Pick up a few acres of land for a song, plant some tomatoes and corn and zucchini, bring in a few chickens and ducks and maybe a cow or two and, presto, you've got instant survival.

This is quite an idyllic scenario, one which is appealing to an increasing number of educated, affluent people each year. But one of the main reasons there is a move back to the land in this country is that the political clout of the nation's traditional farmers has managed to keep the tax and business aspects of farming sacred in the eyes of Congress. Hence, there are many good tax breaks available to someone who wishes to indulge in one's passion for the land, while preserving as much of one's capital as possible from the scythe of the Internal Revenue Service.

Farming, per se, encompasses many varied activities which receive substantial tax breaks, and generate jobs and revenues crucial to local economies. This is, of course, in addition to the products of the land which are consumed on the nation's and world's tables. There are a variety of ways to become a Gentleman Farmer, and enjoy a bumper crop of tax breaks, without actually soiling one's hands. However, many advisors caution that you've got to take a definite active interest in your farming affairs if you wish to qualify for the tax breaks which will be explained in this section—or else the IRS will do ungentlemanly things with your tax return.

The interest in farming—and its components such as livestock breeding, feeding, and racing—as a tax shelter is rising for a number of reasons. For one thing, in many parts of the country, it's fairly easy to finance the purchase of a farm or livestock. Secondly, farmland and breeding stock have proved to be valuable inflation hedges over the past several years. Then, of course, there are all the little loopholes among the meadow muffins which city slickers find so appetizing as they graze through the possibilities.

Losses generated by farming activities can offset taxable income from any other source, says Dick Stone, a partner in the accounting firm of Main Hurdman &

Cranstoun, New York City. However, you do have to prove that you're operating in a businesslike manner to show the IRS that you're not engaged in a hobby. Normally, you must show a profit in at least two out of a five-year cycle (if you raise livestock, it's two out of seven; we'll look at that further in the next chapter). But this can be a fuzzy point, says Stone, who notes that the Tax Court has ruled that it sometimes takes upwards of 15 years to build a breeding herd, for example, to the point of profitability.

On the other hand, the Tax Court itself can be confused on the issue at times. Take, for example, the case which follows: Late in 1979, two Tax Courts in California, ruling on separate but nearly identical cases, reached precisely opposite conclusions in their interpretation of Section 183(a) of the Tax Code of 1954. A dentist in Santa Clara was allowed his expenses on the show horses he raised as a business because it appeared to the judge that the man engaged in an activity for profit. Yet a doctor in Long Beach in nearly the same horse business (the breeds were different, that's all), who kept exactly the same kinds of records, was denied his business losses because the judge interpreted Section 183(a) differently from his upstate colleague—this despite the fact that the doctor's records clearly showed he *attempted* to make a profit in at least two out of any given seven years. The fact that the doctor lost over $120,000 in 11 years trying to improve his breed in order to make a profit apparently did not impress the Long Beach judge. Either that, or the judge didn't like doctors.

It's quite probable that one of those California cases will be overturned someday, although what will probably happen is that the IRS will appeal Santa Clara, the doctor, Long Beach; *both* appeals will be sustained, and we'll be right back where we started.

This Section 183(a) business, however, comes down hardest on the IRS, for the Service is charged with the task of proving that a taxpayer's farming activity is *not* a business if it indeed shows a profit every so often within the guidelines. On the other hand, the taxpayer has to prove it's a business, not a hobby, if no profit is shown during the five or seven-year cycles. Dick Stone has given us some guidelines at the end of this chapter which should make things easier for the taxpayer's case.

You can get into farming by buying and running a farm yourself (true Gentleman Farming) or by participating in cattle, horse, or "aquaculture" deals involving the breeding of everything from catfish to abalone. Let's look at what it takes to go it alone.

Pick an aspect of farming that most appeals to you before considering any investment. That could take a lot of time, investigation, and soul-searching. "Most of the Gentleman Farmers I know spend about two years studying the business before they get into it," says Stone. Learn all you can about crop tillage, marketing, cash flow, weather patterns, and so on. *This is crucial to your investment and your tax strategy*, says Stone. If the farm can support a variety of activities, you then have the advantage of swinging with market demands, thus hedging against losses you might suffer when certain commodity prices plunge. That will also help show the IRS that you're operating in a businesslike manner, that you know wheat from chaff, so to speak.

Generally, farms are fairly easy to finance. In fact, you may even be able to do it through the current owner, with a purchase-money mortgage. A typical deal would involve a 29% down payment, and a 15-year balloon mortgage. You'd pay interest only for the first five years at perhaps 10-12%, all of which is deductible. After the fifth year, you'd pay interest and principal.

Bank financing can be arranged in many parts of the country, but don't expect a bank located in a city far from the country to be too sympathetic to your needs. Deal with a local bank in the area where you are searching for land. In fact, you might be able to qualify for a program available under the Federal Land Bank, which will lend you up to 85% of the land's value. But as with most bureaucracies, whether the FLB will even consider financing a Gentleman Farm often depends on the local administrator. They're very active in some areas; openly antagonistic in others.

You can buy a reasonable spread in some parts of the country for very little money. A good place to start looking is in the most recent catalogue issued by such national farm-bank real estate agencies as United Farm (612 West 47 Street, Kansas City, Mo. 64112). These agencies have offices all over the country, and their catalogues (which are free) list everything from 120-acre horse ranches in Colorado to hay farms in New York to almond spreads in California to cattle kingdoms in Texas. Lots of dreams pass before you as you flip through the pages of these books.

There are two significant tax breaks in farming which make it a highly attractive shelter, says Dick Stone. First, there are all the up-front deductions you can take for depreciation, the 10% investment tax credit, operating expenses, and interest payments. Second, these write-offs, if not substantial, when recaptured, may now be treated as long-term capital gains (taxed at maximum 28%) rather than ordinary income (up to 70% tax rate).

You can depreciate equipment, barns, silos, and any income-producing property on the farm to build your tax shelter. And you can usually assign a value to each of those components based on the total purchase price of the farm. That can often add up to a substantial portion of the total farm purchase price. For example, say the farm has two residences—a main house and a smaller facility for the staff. You can depreciate the assigned value of the second house if you rent it out to the staff or allow them to use it free in return for their services.

If you plan to raise livestock, you can depreciate their costs over a period of years—depending on the "useful life" of those animals. For example, a nine-year-old horse can be depreciated over five years, but a thirteen-year-old can be depreciated over three years (see tables in next chapter).

Operating costs are fully deductible in the year they're implemented and paid. That includes the cost of manager and crew to run the farm, planting and harvesting crops, feeding animals, and so on. If you need new equipment, you can take a 10% investment tax credit on it in the year you buy it as well as deduct the interest on the loan you took out to buy the equipment.

There's even more shelter—and cash flow—to be had if you decide not to live on the property at all, but leave it in the hands of a competent manager. It all has to do with the increasing interest in "country life" vacations. Here's how it works: Say that farm has a 16-room main residence, where the manager and his family will live. You could convert some of the rooms into guest facilities and rent them to city folk who want a country vacation. You can then take accelerated depreciation on the cost of the house, and possibly some of its furnishings. Remember, though, as owner you cannot live in this main house for 14 days or more during any year. If you do, you'll lose this tax break. However, you can always use a cottage on the farm for your own purposes.

You might be best off taking one of these country vacations yourself before deciding whether or not the Gentleman Farming business is for you. An excellent guide to check out is *Farm, Ranch & Country Vacations,* available for $5.95, from Farm & Ranch Vacations, 36 East 57th Street, New York, N.Y. 10022.

Here are some challenge-tested guidelines to follow to prove to the IRS that you're in business for a profit when it comes to farming. They're provided by Dick Stone, of Main Hurdman & Cranstoun.

1. *Operate like a business.* Change your operating methods in response to economic conditions. If the price of corn drops, and soybeans are rising, plant soybeans.

2. *Seek and use the advice of experts.* Hire a manager, or keep the old owner around to supervise things. Spend time on the farm looking after your business.

3. *Keep accurate records.* Set up a professional book-keeping system, monitor results, keep breeding records up-to-date, maintain local bank accounts.

4. *Show that you expect to make money* by keeping tabs on, and recording, rising land values, market values for animals, etc.

5. *Demonstrate that you're a smart businessperson in your other interests.* If you own another business, or are a successful corporate manager, show the entrepreneurial side of your nature in your farming activities.

6. *Show that you actually have taken time to make this a profitable business* by improving the property, replacing old equipment, getting the best deal for your crops or animals.

7. *Above all, be able to prove that the farm is not a recreational venture* for you and your family, says Stone.

That means don't get carried away with putting in swimming pools, tennis courts, polo fields, etc. Take the land as nature has given it to you, work it, and try to make a buck out of the deal. You'll be surprised at how much you can "lose" by gaining.

18.

Whinny Whinny, Neigh Neigh: Tax Shelters On The Hoof

If it's true that money makes the mare go 'round, you wouldn't *believe* what's going on in the breeding sheds of America's horse farms. Since 1973, when great gobs of foreign money started to come into the American horse markets, the price for top quality Thoroughbred horses has literally outpaced the rate of inflation and helped revitalize an industry which had fallen on dull times. Of course, 1973 was also the year of Secretariat, a genuine equine superstar; and racing has subsequently benefited from a parade of exciting horses such as Affirmed, Seattle Slew, Spectacular Bid, and Genuine Risk to keep both the public appetite for the sport whetted, and investors' wallets open.

But the real attraction for many new investors in Thoroughbred horses is the neat tax shelter it affords. An investor in racehorses can deduct the cost of feeding, maintaining, and training a horse to race—or keeping a stallion or mare for breeding purposes. Moreover, you can take depreciation on both racing and breeding stock. How much you can take, and the write-off you get as a result, depend upon an animal's age.

The combination of foreign money, tax shelter, and high purses at racetracks has helped make Thorough-bred racing (and harness and quarter horse racing as well) one of the most glamorous tax shelters around. "It sure as hell beats watching a building depreciate," is the way one of the industry's most successful syndicators, W. Cothran Campbell of Dogwood Farm, Atlanta, puts it. However, it's also one of the trickiest investments you can make. Nature, animal temperaments, and some-times swiftly changing market conditions dictated by breeding fashions can make or break your investment. Even so, there are enough people willing to "take the gamble" in this country. So many, in fact, that Thor-oughbred racing now probably amounts to a $4 billion per year industry worldwide—larger than either the mo-tion picture or recording business, according to most estimates.

Whether you're interested in Thoroughbreds or harness or quarter horses, the general tax and invest-ment rules are basically the same. We're going to use Thoroughbred examples in this chapter for a few reasons: more states offer Thoroughbred racing and have state-sponsored breeding programs than either harness or quarter horse racing; the sport receives far more attention in the media than either of the other two forms of racing; the people involved in the business and sporting ends are more varied, ranging from queens and princes to sheiks and cattle barons to the landed gentry and upstart entrepreneurs; and, most important, I like Thoroughbreds better than harness or quarter horses.

Purses in racing are climbing all the time (as are ex-penses). But interest in the sport has become so great that many novices spend literally millions each year to buy unproven horses. In 1979, for example, Sy Weintraub, chairman of Columbia Pictures, made his first investment in the business, co-signing with a partner for 16 untested yearling horses to the tune of over $6 million. They purchased their horses at auction from one Nelson Bunker Hunt, who has had just as much influence in driving up the price of racing and breeding stock as he did on silver. And Weintraub is only a drop in the bucket. In 1977, around 5,000 yearlings were sold at public auction for a little over $83 million. By the time 1980 came along, this figure had nearly *doubled*. In the three major summer sales held in Kentucky and Saratoga each year, the price of an average yearling has jumped from $35,000 in 1975 to well over $170,000. That's not only keeping ahead of inflation, it's also establishing a higher depreciation base for someone else —because as long as a horse remains a viable racing commodity and can be saved for breeding purposes, its value is likely to increase dramatically every year, and people with big bucks to spend can offset their breeding risks with high depreciation if they buy the horse for stud purposes.

The object is to develop stakes winners—for immediate return as well as breeding value. If a filly becomes a stakes winner, her value soars as a broodmare and she can be sold to commercial breeders for a huge profit. Or, you could breed her yourself to a string of high-priced stallions and get a string of very marketable yearlings to sell. If a broodmare foals a stakes winner, her value—and the value of her sisters and brothers—rise just as quickly. (Geldings, on the other hand, are eunuchs, and can only be used to race.)

Horse racing can be an "either/or" business: either you lose money and are a fool, or you make money and are a good businessperson; when it's in between, you're a true sportsman or sportswoman. A case in point is Harry Meyerhoff, a real estate developer from Maryland who'd been racing horses with moderate success over the years, but nothing too spectacular had come his way in all that time. Until 1977, that is, when he successfully bid $37,000 at auction for a grey yearling colt with a good sire (Bold Bidder) and a fairly interesting (but nonstakes - producing) dam (Spectacular). Meyerhoff named his horse Spectacular Bid, and all he did was win America's Triple Crown, earn more than $2 million in purses, and get syndicated in 40 shares for stud duty for a cool $22 million. Nice return on investment, eh? The beauty of it all is that this horse has been a tax shelter on the hoof (as well as coronary inducer) for most of his career.

Of course, things can work the other way. Of all the yearlings sold at auction since 1960 for $250,000 or more, only about a dozen have justified their investment on the track or in the breeding shed thus far. One nag, Canadian Bound, sired by the aforementioned Secretariat, cost $1.5 million as a yearling; he didn't earn more than a few thousand dollars in two years of racing.

If you want to get into Thoroughbred racing, there are at least a dozen or so ways one can go about taking the plunge. However, all the rules listed in the previous chapter in this section apply double for these types of investments, because in this business, you're just as likely to be taken by a sharp operator than in any other tax shelter. It's not that racing is dishonest; as a matter of fact, it's probably the cleanest sport around, occasional scandals about fixing and doping notwithstanding. Mr. Campbell of Dogwood Farm, who's been in more than his share of glamorous businesses over the years, says that the finest people he's ever been around are in racing. "You can look a man in the eye, shake his hand, and seal a deal which will stick," he says. And Campbell should

know. Since 1973, when he started his unique operation
of racing syndications, he's put over 300 high tax
bracket investors into more than 70 limited partnerships
involving horses worth more than $20 million. He's
made a few mistakes and bought a few turkeys, but
those he chalks up as the breaks of the game. His horses
have also won a good deal of money over the years—and
more than 70% of his partnerships have either broken
even or made money, after tax considerations, compared
to the nearly 85% of all racehorse owners who *lose*
money each year.

Campbell is a success because he knows his business
and knows what he's doing. The same is true of Meyerhoff, Nelson Bunker Hunt, the landed gentry like the
Whitneys, Mellons, Gerrys, Vanderbilts, and Phippses,
and neophytes who come into the sport and wind up
owning major stakes winners right off the bat. These
people are prepared, they have studied the business, the
horses, the bloodlines, the patterns; they have garnered
good advice; and they all have a deep love for the
animals involved. "Unless an investor has an appreciation for the *horse*, he probably won't make a go of this
game," says Campbell.

Personally, I have found that education both on and
off the track and the farms is the best way to go. Read
the trade publications religiously. These would include
the *Daily Racing Form*, the only sports national daily in
the country, with a circulation of 150,000, and a cover
price of $1.75; two slick weekly magazines, *The Blood-
Horse* (Box 4038, Lexington, Ky. 40544, $62.50 per
year), and *The Thoroughbred Record* (Box 11788, Lexington, Ky. 40505, $50 per year); plus a neat insider's
newsletter, *Racing Update* (Box 11052, Lexington, Ky.
40512, $100 per year). And you thought New York City
was the publishing capital of the world? You will find
just about everything from race results to economic
trends to tax treatments to breeding advice in the pages

of these publications. You would also do well to invest $12 in a remarkable 175-page paperback, *How To Make Money Investing in Thoroughbreds* (CCS Publishing, Box 982, Covington, La. 70433). Ghost-written for Jack Lohman, owner of Clear Creek Stud in Folsom, La., and published by him, this is the only tome I've ever read which lays out all the details a novice (or an experienced fan, but neophyte investor) should know about the economics, tax advantages, and heartaches of the business.

The most common way to invest in Thoroughbreds is to buy a horse, or a string of steeds, on your own, and then to pump thousands of dollars into developing a first-class operation. You don't have to be on the Big Apple circuit in New York/New Jersey/Maryland, or in California and Kentucky and Florida to do so; there are plenty of opportunities in Ohio, Michigan, Illinois, Nebraska, Washington, Louisiana, Pennsylvania, and other states with race tracks and breeding industries.

Since 1973, however, a new form of investing has taken hold which is basically structured along the lines of all other tax shelters—the limited partnership, in which an experienced entrepreneur brings a few people together for the purposes of spreading the risk in a racing or breeding operation. The two best known of these kinds of new investment vehicles are those run by Cot Campbell of Dogwood Farm, and those organized by Thomas A. Martin of Kinderhill Farm, Old Chatham, New York.

I've known Campbell since he decided to leave his post as founder and chairman of one of Atlanta's premiere ad agencies to plunge full-time into the business he knows and loves best, racing. Tom Martin, although I know him for a shorter period of time, has also proven to be a good judge of horseflesh and a successful entrepreneur in the business. Campbell basically races horses; Martin races some horses, but primarily organizes his limited partnerships as breeding ventures, to take advantage of the lucrative New York State Breeders Fund program spreading like wildfire in the Empire State. Both men charge markups on their activities, and, at times, they can be substantial; but in racing, which is a high overhead business, these markups are part of the trade. Both also leverage their investments, and in some cases their limited partners are at-risk for the notes they sign. However, each horse is usually insured for its full market value, so that if anything goes wrong, like a broken leg, lightning striking, or sterility, the investors' downside risks are minimized.

Both Campbell and Martin take full advantage of the depreciation schedules assigned to the useful lives of the horses they purchase, and Campbell reports that write-offs of 150% of one's cash investment are not uncommon. As for economic return, Martin flatly states that a 10% annual return in the business "is easy, if you know what you're doing. We wouldn't be in the business if we couldn't achieve at least that objective." Martin, by the way, is also president of American Asset Management, and used to run the $2 billion Anchor Fund at one time.

Under ERTA, the depreciation schedules for horses have been simplified to avoid IRS challenges on the matter. Some in the industry are not too happy about the changes; others see an opportunity for creative investors to massage the new tax laws to better advantage. It basically boils down to a question of the age and use of the horse(s) in your portfolio, and when your tax year begins and ends.

Let's get the problem of a horse's age and use out of the way first. There are two types of Thoroughbred "uses": race horses and those held for breeding. A race horse is one in training, or halter-broken, and is being prepped for his fling at the races. Yearlings being prepped to race (horses do not begin their careers until they're two years old), and most other steeds through the age of five or six, are considered race horses. Many geldings (a neutered male horse) race until they drop, but the general pattern is to race a male or female for no more than three or four years and then retire them to the breeding shed.

Once retired, a male horse (stallion) can frolic through the female (broodmare) herd for many years, some, like the venerable Nashua, moving right along until age 30, when, presumably, he expired with a smile on his face. (In human terms, that was equivalent to 90 years of age, and he looked better than some joggers I know.) Females generally can produce a foal a year through their 20th year if they are exceptionally fertile and durable. The great Secretariat, for example, was produced by a mare who was 21 years old at the time she gave birth.

In both racing and breeding, the length of time you have to depreciate the horse depends on the age of the animal at the time of acquisition. The older the horse at the time of purchase, the more liberal the depreciation rules—ostensibly because the horse's useful life at the time of purchase is shortened. "Older" horses are defined somewhat nebulously by ERTA, and the IRS has yet to rule on a critical bit of wording in the law which could present a tax trap to very aggressive investors. Briefly, the law states that horses held for *racing* can be depreciated over a three-year period, and horses held for breeding over the same time, if they are "more than" two or twelve years old, respectively, at the time of purchase. Otherwise, a five-year depreciation rule applies.

The problem is that all horses have a universal birthday—January 1—regardless of when they were foaled during the year. Thus, a horse can technically be "more than" two or twelve years old on January 2, 1985, even if it was foaled on May 1, 1983, or May 1, 1973. The IRS hasn't quite decided the right birthday ruling yet, and meanwhile, a bit of confusion reigns in the industry. Many owners are opting to go with the January 2 interpretation, which, if denied by the IRS, would result in penalty deficiency payments, though these are not thought to be substantial.

Here are the depreciation schedules:

FOR RACE HORSES MORE THAN TWO YEARS OLD AND BREEDING STOCK MORE THAN TWELVE

Depreciation Year	% of Depreciation
One	25%
Two	38%
Three	37%

ALL OTHER HORSES

One	15%
Two	22%
Three, Four, Five	21% each

It's apparent, then, that the tax advantage lies with the horse purchased at an older age. However, there are tremendous pitfalls for the investor who decides to enter Thoroughbred racing strictly to take advantage of the more liberal depreciation schedule for older horses. In the case of older broodmares and stallions, there is the chance that complications of age could compromise the economic factors of the business—a mare could prove difficult to get in foal the older she gets, or could abort more easily; a stallion could experience problems in potency as he gets on in years. It doesn't always happen this way, but there is that chance.

If you purchase older racing stock, the chances of injury might increase with age (especially if you have a dumb trainer), or the horse may "sour" during its fifth or sixth year. In that case, you could still continue to depreciate the horse over a three-year period if you send it off to a breeding shed. Many race-horse owners, however, do not like the breeding business—it's an extremely competitive, sometimes high-cost endeavor subject to market whims—and prefer to sell their race horses to professional breeders. This can complicate tax matters somewhat for the neophyte investor, so you'd be well advised to have an experienced bloodstock agent or managing agent handling your Thoroughbred affairs to counsel you not only on bloodlines, conformation, racing potential, and breeding possibilities, but also on the various tax aspects associated with all these endeavors.

You can obtain decent tax benefits, however, if you use leverage to finance your Thoroughbred purchases. Remember, you will have to be at-risk for the loans involved in order to take advantage of the depreciation— and the tax year may have to begin on January 1 in order to take full depreciation no matter when the horse is purchased. This is a very important factor to consider, especially if you're wooed by one of the many promoters who've suddenly come into this game offering syndications geared strictly to tax consequences. That's because if the syndicate's tax year doesn't begin until July 1, for example, you will be allowed only one-half the depreciation (or 1/12th for every month) if the tax year ends December 31. Hence, you would be well advised to begin your Thoroughbred operations in January in order to take advantage of depreciation. Then, you'd have all year to look for the best prospects, even purchasing them in December, and taking the full year's depreciation.

Let's look at an example of how leverage and depreciation can add up to tax shelter in a well-structured Thoroughbred deal. We'll use a four-horse package, consisting of a three-year-old filly in training, a four-

year-old colt, and two 13-year-old broodmares in foal.
Total package cost for the animals would amount to
$400,000 ($100,000 each), and there would be 10 investors in the program. (In most states, no more than 10
separate interests can own a race horse.) The package
would be managed by experienced horse people, so there
would be fees involved. Training costs would amount to
$1,500 per month for the filly and colt, and boarding
costs $500 per month for the broodmares.

The filly would be purchased in January, the colt in
July, and the broodmares in November. There would be
a 5% bloodstock commission and 10% management fee
based on the price of the horses. Insurance on the filly
and colt would be 7% of the purchase price per year, 4%
on the broodmares. Bank loans—or, better yet, seller-
financing—amounting to 75% of the purchase price, 20%
interest only the first year, would be included in the
package. The investors would be responsible for insurance, training, and board costs out of pocket for three
years assuming no racing or breeding income accrued to
the partnership. Here's the way the numbers would look:

	Three-year Costs	First-year Cash
NON-DEDUCTIBLE		
Filly purchase price	$100,000	$ 25,000
Colt purchase price	100,000	25,000
Broodmare price	200,000	50,000

(continued on p. 180)

	Three-year Costs	First-year Cash
DEDUCTIBLE		
Insurance, race horses	52,000	10,500*
Insurance, broodmares	24,000	1,300*
Training, race horses	90,000	27,000*
Board, broodmares	36,000	2,000*
Stud fees	50,000	—
Bloodstock commission	20,000	20,000
Management fee	30,000	30,000
Interest, 3 years	120,000	60,000**
TOTAL CASH	$822,000	$250,800
Deductible Expenses	$422,000	$150,800
Depreciation	400,000	100,000
TOTAL DEDUCTIONS	$822,000	$250,800

Cash per unit, first year: $25,000
Write-off per unit $25,800, or 103%

After-tax dollars invested: $25,000 less 50% of $25,800 equals $12,100

While these numbers may seem large and somewhat complicated, there is another form of investment in Thoroughbreds taking hold, largely as a result of the efforts of Fasig-Tipton Co., Inc., the Thoroughbred auction sales company headquartered in Elmont, N.Y. Through its subsidiary, Thoroughbred Equity Company (Teco), an investor interested in getting into racing and breeding can arrange to *lease* one or more fillies for a maximum period of six years—a program designed to spread the cash risk evenly over a period of time for the lessee and provide a steady income, and return of the fil-

*pro-rated as of purchase date during year
**interest payable in advance, first year

ly for breeding purposes, for the lessor (or owner or breeder).

Here's how it works: Say, you're interested in buying three yearling fillies but realize the price for the package will be $150,000. You don't want to leverage yourself to the hilt, and you're really only looking for a 100% write-off of your investment. Teco will arrange a lease program wherein you pay 24 quarterly installments of $6,562 for the use of those fillies over a six-year period. That's equal to $150,000 plus a 5% monitoring fee—there is no interest cost on the lease. You place the fillies in training, race them, pay for all the costs of training and insurance, keep their winnings on the race track— and have the opportunity to breed them through their seventh year, keeping all the foals produced, plus the foal *in utero* at the time the lease expires. This effectively keeps your cash-flow under control for a stated period of time and returns the "proven" broodmares to the breeder, who goes into this arrangement in order to guarantee a return of a quality mare to his breeding program.

Similarly, you could purchase a group of fillies from a breeder and lease them to other investors yourself under the Teco program—something some savvy investors are beginning to discover gives them depreciation advantages without the headaches of operating a racing or breeding establishment. Michael Lischin, vice-president of Teco, will give you all the details of this program—and help you out in other matters relating to investing in Thoroughbreds—if you give him a jingle at 516-328-1800.

You would think that a simple thing like a horse would be one of the easiest tax shelter investments to understand. Unfortunately, this Sport of Kings has become overrun with Captains of Industry during the last decade or so, and the rules have changed dramatically in the market. As a result, it's a much more competitive business, with huge sums of money changing hands every day in an effort to corner the market on fashionable bloodlines. The unwary investor who plunges right into the business without seeking out solid advice is likely to wind up with a bad case of hoof-in-wallet disease.

Racing can be the most exciting of tax shelters—or the most disappointing, depending on how you structure your own goals to conform with the present market conditions. The tax rewards are there for the taking; the economic rewards can be achieved with sound management and a bit of good fortune; and the thrill of watching your horse struggle across the finish line to win even the most insignificant race can add up to a heck of a lot more fun than sticking your finger in the ground in Ohio and watching the gas fizz up.

Besides, there's just no better place to spend a lazy August afternoon than hobnobbing with the Vanderbilts in the owners' boxes at Saratoga. My daughter has an expression for it: "It's just so, oh, well . . . pish-posh!"

19.

Once Upon A Time There Was A Moo-Cow Come Down The Road...

You can wait until the cows come home before you're likely to get a definitive answer on the economics involved in tax shelters involving cattle. The popularity of cattle feeding as a tax shelter has undergone more peaks and valleys than any other kind of tax-related investment, for a host of economic and tax reasons. Now, to add to the confusion, there are indications that a new boom in moo-cow shelters may be upon us—in dairy herds, as opposed to previous emphasis on cattle raised for slaughter.

Thus, we'll be talking in this chapter of two different kinds of cattle investments—those which put meat on the table, and those which put milk in the bottle. Both have their risks on the operating end, and each could present tax problems for the investor who's not paying too much attention to what's going on in the marketplace.

First of all, cattle feeding is not strictly a tax shelter. Most advisors prefer to think of this activity as strictly a tax-deferral maneuver which should only be considered by those who have an absolute minimum of $50,000 to $100,000 in loose change lying around. In most cases, these would be people who—through inheritance, windfall profits, or employment bonuses—wind up with far too much taxable income in one particular year to plan for a truly comprehensive annual tax-shelter portfolio. Many of these people consider cattle feeding because it can give you a 100% tax deduction in the year of investment, during which time you can plan more effectively on how to diversify a true tax-shelter portfolio based on the income generated the following year from the sale of cattle. All your deductions in cattle feeding are merely deferred until the time you sell—at which point the deferrals are recaptured at ordinary income tax rates. Since this can be a very short cycle, the *timing* of a cattle feeding investment is extremely crucial. You don't want to invest too early in the year, or else you may wind up selling in the same year—too late in the calendar to shelter your gains, if any.

The write-offs in cattle feeding come from the cost of fattening a herd of cattle for market—that's your actual cash investment including the cost of grain, feedlot operations, etc. You acquire the cattle through bank financing. The interest on the loan is deductible, and the amount of your loan is used to figure your basis when calculating profits, or losses, when the cattle are sold for slaughter. However, the cattle cannot be depreciated because they are for feeding, not breeding, purposes.

You can leverage your investment and get a higher tax break by also financing the costs of feeding. For example, if it costs $300,000 to feed 1,500 cows, you might put up $100,000 and borrow the rest. But if you're an individual investor, you can only do this on a recourse basis—where you're at-risk by being liable for the loan.

You could then deduct the full $300,000 if the feed is consumed in the year purchased. Private corporations which are not closely held might be able to finance these deals on a nonrecourse basis and take the deduction if the economic outlook is promising.

The economics of cattle feeding, however, is not simply a matter of what sirloin is going for down at Safeway. The first thing you should look for in any cattle deal is the price per head of the cattle being purchased. Unlike the horse market, where bloodlines make a difference, feeder cattle prices are fairly uniform at any particular time; they can be found in the commodity tables of the daily newspapers. If the price you're being asked to pay for cattle is well above the prevailing rates, the deal probably won't make much sense economically—especially if the IRS takes a peek.

You might hear some promoter trying to use the excuse that there's a shortage of feeder cattle coming up in the future, and the prices are bound to go up to cover your investment. Take this advice with a large salt block. Cattle prices have fluctuated wildly during the past decade, and not always because of the supply/demand factor. While it's true that beef boycotts led to some reduction in herds, that did not necessarily make the remaining cows more profitable when they came to market. Why? The price of grain, of marketing, of labor, of energy—crucial ingredients to a feedlot operator—have all gotten out of hand as well. In addition, bank financing charges can eat into the profitability of a herd substantially.

On the other hand, competition from pork and poultry producers has helped ease the per capita demand on beef recently. It's much cheaper for a family to serve pork or chicken than beef, and in times of high inflation, beef can suffer at the hands of a squeezed shopper. Many promoters like to point to the rising consumption of beef in fast-food outlets as a reason which should keep demand, and prices, moving up, if not steady. What they fail to tell you, however, is that many beef chains raise their own feeder cattle, and hedge their bets in the commodity markets as well. This "demand" may be a bit false when it comes to having an effect on the market price for cattle.

How widely can beef prices fluctuate? According to Larry Feldman, president of Taurus Corporation of Boulder, Colorado, prices for cattle were about $78 per head at market in April of 1979; they then dropped to around $60 by July, and stayed in that range until early 1980, when they started moving slowly above the $70 range. By November 1981 the price had plummeted once again to close to $60. Clearly, this is a volatile market, with the costs of feeding not getting any lower, and the price of the product subject to the price of the competition, weather, consumer demand, and a variety of other factors.

Hence, you need a competent manager to advise you on cattle feeding investments. Feldman of Taurus suggests you might seek out the advice of large bank trust departments which are used to feeding cattle for their clients as part of a year-round tax planning strategy. One of the questions to ask the promoter or manager is how much it can really cost to fatten a herd for market. The answer you should get, according to Feldman, is "a pound of gain for 10 times the cost of one pound of grain." Thus, it should cost 40 cents to put a pound on one steer if the current average price of a pound of grain is four cents (10 times four cents). To check out the prevailing feed costs in the newspaper quotes, divide the price per bushel quoted by 56 to get the price per pound.

As mentioned, you must time this kind of investment to correspond with your tax situation. If you must defer your losses to another year, try to start feeding

cattle between the beginning of June and the beginning
of August. This will allow you to write off the full allot-
ment of feed and maintenance costs, and get your cattle
to market in the beginning of the next calendar year. If
you feed after August, you probably won't be able to
deduct all your costs in the year you need the write-offs.

Even though cattle feeding usually is a six-to-nine-
month activity (and selling the cattle is at the discretion
of the feedlot operator, not the investor), the fluctuations in maintenance and cattle prices can still be
frighteningly large. You're dealing in commodities which
are traded on futures markets—cattle and grain—and
even relatively small swings in grain and beef futures
could affect a cattle feeding investment. Rather than
trying to beat the futures markets, you should consider
a program which relies heavily on hedging in the futures
market. It's a good way of cutting down the risks of a
substantial loss—and assuring potential profits. If you
can lock in what appears to be a reasonable profit by
hedging (selling live cattle futures contracts), take it,
and don't risk a drop in the market which could cause a
loss. This is a tax shelter which can give you more indigestion on paper than a slightly tainted steak can give
you in some backwater Sloppy Joe's.

If cattle feeding is a turbulent deal, milking
cows—or dairy farming—is precisely the opposite. "This
is a deal in which nothing happens," says Dave Kassel,
president of Agricultural Asset Management, a pioneer
in this still minor tax shelter. "No oil well is going to
come in, no one's going to make a fortune," Kassel continues. But there are some interesting tax and investment considerations of this kind of cattle deal, not the
least of which is the fact that the cash investment required is closer to $35,000, and the write-offs can exceed
100% of your cash investment.

I must stress in this chapter that dairy farming shelters are a relatively new concept, developed primarily by

Kassel. Since it's basically a boring field, a lot of promoters have yet to discover it. Like most shelters involving commodities, dairy farming requires intensive day-to-day management which an investor should entrust to a competent, experienced promoter. My research indicates that these deals may eventually wind up on the shelves of a lot of stockbrokers' offices because large corporate farmers have discovered the possibilities recently. They have the clout to organize and market these deals through major brokerage firms. If this comes to pass, be very careful about the fees and commissions you will be asked to pay, or the economics may not work out.

Basically, when you get into dairy farming, you're helping out an established farmer by purchasing a herd of cows and calves, and leasing them back to the farmer. This is a relatively stable business without the sharp ups and downs of most agricultural commodities because the price of milk and milk products is guaranteed by the Federal Government. Every day the product goes to market at the basic federal price, and twice a month the full production of a farm is paid for by government programs. This, says Kassel, is good and bad news—depending on one's outlook. While there's always a market for milk (and a fixed price), a dairy farmer has not got a shot at a bonanza year because his capital is tied up in overhead.

"It's difficult for a farmer to expand his herd because his carrying costs would go up," says Kassel. He'd need more barn space, more milking machines, and more cows, much of which has to be financed by banks. Cutting back on a herd is also tough because prior financing charges are paid off through milk production, and the less milk a farmer sells, the less cash generated to pay off the bank. "A dairy farmer is locked in because his investment in each animal is so significant, working out to around $4,000 per cow in overhead over a seven-year life, only five of which years are productive," continues Kassel. It's no surprise, then, that the number of farms and cows has declined recently, although productivity per cow has risen. "The bottom line in this business is you either get big, or go out of business, especially if you're a young farmer just starting out," Kassel says.

Because the operating margin is so low in milk production anyway, a dairy farmer usually can't take full advantage of the depreciation schedules for a herd, even when leverage is taken into consideration. The dairy farmer's constant need is for fresh capital, and the concept worked out by Kassel's firm seems to work fairly equitably.

Investors in dairy farming generally purchase the current herd of cows on a farm, and lease them back to the farmer. This generates cash to the farmer, who can then go ahead and build new facilities or acquire more land. The same investors, or another group, then purchase the cows to utilize those facilities, and lease them to the farmer as well. The farmer keeps all but about 18% of the milk proceeds to service the overhead of his operations, and to continue expansion programs.

The investor—as owner of the cows—gets all the tax advantages of depreciation on a herd and leverage, plus income with which to pay off the financing required to obtain the herd. At the end of the seven-year cycle, the investor sells the herd for the same price as he or she bought it or higher. How, you ask, can you sell a herd of dairy cows that has been milked dry, so to speak, if the useful life is only five years? The answer lies in the fact that the farmer has been culling the herd over the years, disposing of males (for veal), and older heifers, keeping female calves, and replacing fully depreciated animals with new in-use cows. Thus, if the average cost of a cow in a herd purchased in 1981 is $1,200, the chances are that in 1988, adjusted for inflation, that herd will be sold for at least that price, and probably more, since the composition of the herd will be basically the same kinds of animals purchased in 1981.

The tax shelter involved is rather simple—with one tax bugaboo not yet resolved by the IRS. Say it costs $30,000 for a herd. The investor puts up $7,500 (25%) in cash, and signs a seven-year recourse note with a bank (not the promoter; the investor is on the hook to a real financial institution). The investor also pays a fairly hefty management fee to the promoter, which, if the deal is structured properly, can be 100% deductible in the year of investment. Sometimes this fee can equal in cash outlay the initial down payment for the herd.

The investor then takes depreciation on the herd, plus the interest charges. In addition, since the investor is leasing the cows to the farmer, a 10% investment tax credit is taken in the first year by the investor. The investment tax credit situation is the one sticky point of these deals, according to some advisors, because the IRS may determine that the investor is in the dairy business, not the leasing business, and thus be ineligible for the 10% credit. As of press time, there has been no ruling on this matter from the boys and girls in Washington, D.C., but one should pay careful attention to this potential pitfall if considering a dairy shelter.

What the investor gets for approximately $15,000 in cash (the down payment plus the management fee) is a depreciable herd of cows, a note amortizing at the bank, and enough cash flow based on federal price supports to cover that financing, plus a return of about 9% per year after taxes based on the portion of the milk receipts not used for retiring the debt. At the end of seven years, the cows are sold by the promoter, at a profit, a portion of which may be long-term capital gain.

This seems like a fairly conservative, and to say the least, liquid, tax shelter which may become more popular in the years ahead. The best way to check out a promoter in these deals is to ask for the names of current or former investors, and to check with them as to whether their tax returns have held up to IRS scrutiny. A chat with the farmers who will keep the cows might also help, since you'll want to get a line on the promoter's reputation within the industry. On the surface, dairy farming looks like one of those deals which has the potential of being as good as ice cream; but one should be careful when strolling through the prospectus so as to avoid the meadow muffins on the tax side.

Part Six

Equipment Leasing: "Pardon Me, Boys ... Is This The Depreciation Choo-Choo?"

20.

Going Out
On A Lease

Equipment leasing is supposed to be the Shelter of the
Eighties, according to many people on Wall Street whom
I've chatted with recently. One of the reasons for this
new enthusiasm is that there is a crying need for plant
and equipment modernization in many industries, and
replacing that obsolete stuff might cost too much. Then,
we seem to be on the verge of an entrepreneurial explo-
sion in this country which will require that many new
businesses find creative ways to acquire the equipment
they need to become competitive in their industry. As a
matter of ironic fact, the last great entrepreneurial era in
America (the 1960s) gave birth to the entire equipment
leasing industry, thanks to the investment tax credit
enacted in 1962.

Now, things have come full circle, it seems. Many investors are discovering that equipment leasing deals don't cost as much as might be expected, are easy to finance, and can generate a nice income as well as a capital gain down the road. And though some aspects of equipment leasing as a tax shelter were fidgeted with by the Tax Reform Act of 1976, there are still some good tax breaks—if the deal is set up correctly.

In theory, at least, leasing deals are simple. An investor buys the equipment from a manufacturer or middleman with a down payment of from 10% to 20%. This is done on a full-recourse basis to avoid the at-risk provisions of the tax law. That means the investor is liable to pay the note off to the finance company if the lease turns sour. To avoid that happening, the investor should arrange to lease the equipment over a period of time to a financially strong organization. The monthly receipts from that lease may be large enough to cover the monthly payments to the bank or finance company and give a modest profit.

Some promoters claim that you can make an annual return of over 8% on your investment in equipment leasing. You probably can—in some deals. It all depends on who structures the deal, how big it is, and who gets what off the top. Most of the leases are on a net-net basis, which means the lessee (user of the equipment) is responsible for picking up the maintenance, supplies, etc.

Almost anybody can set up a leasing deal of his own—with some professional help. For example, a group of doctors could buy radiology equipment and lease it back to a hospital or a professional corporation of radiologists. A few executives could finance the purchase of 10 photocopiers and lease them back to their employer, or even another company. And a group of local merchants might buy a computer and lease time on it to accountants, lawyers, or other merchants—including themselves. The possibilities, in fact, are limited only by the imagination and the availability of OPM (other people's money) to finance the deal.

For their part, users are anxious to enter into leasing agreements for a number of reasons. Some major ones include:

• Many companies can't fully utilize the tax benefits which equipment leasing throws off. They may have low current tax bills, tax loss carry-forwards, or already high depreciation deductions from other investments.

• Lease payments are a cost of doing business, and are deductible; amortization of loan principal is not.

• The user gets 100% financing without putting up any cash, uses the equipment, and saves on capital expenditures.

• Leasing arrangements, done privately, often open the doors to other deals with those same investors. For example, a company could later go back to the investor group and privately place bonds, stock, or mortgages, without having to go "public."

If the deal is structured properly, the investor will get some very nice tax benefits. You can take accelerated depreciation on the equipment, deduct interest on the loan, and possibly even take a 10% investment tax credit on the cost of the equipment.

In real life, of course, this kind of investment scenario is too good for the Tax Kids to leave alone. Hence, equipment leasing is hamstrung by a variety of "whereases and wherefores" which can leave even the most sophisticated attorney cross-eyed.

For one thing, the investment tax credit isn't usually available to individuals or limited partnerships, notes

Bill Brennan, the newsletter publisher. Generally speaking, it's designed for corporations. Individual lessors can take the ITC only if: (1) the term of the lease is for less than half the equipment's useful life; and (2) the lessor's operating costs for the first 12 months of the lease equal 15% or more of the rental income generated by the equipment. Requiring an investor to assume the economic risk of having to find another customer after the first short-term lease ends can scare off a lot of investors, Brennan figures. And the requirement for operating costs to equal 15% of lease revenues is hard to achieve on a net-net lease, where the user absorbs these costs. There still are, however, ways in which an individual can take tax credit—especially in railroad cars, which have been a glamour investment since the late 1970s. We'll look at the choo-choo shelters later on in this chapter.

Deducting accelerated depreciation may also be a problem because it can trigger the 15% minimum tax on tax preference items. The minimum tax is figured on the difference between straight-line and accelerated depreciation, as well as other preference items. Straight-line depreciation does not trigger the 15% minimum, however. How important this is depends upon your own situation and, perhaps, on the way the deal is structured. The difference in deductions can be substantial. If a $100,000 piece of equipment has a five-year useful life (industry standards are applied for each type of equipment), taking straight-line depreciation would give you a $20,000 write-off each year ($100,000 ÷ 5). By contrast, accelerated depreciation on the same piece of equipment could give you a first-year's deduction of $40,000. Depending on your tax bracket, the example above could mean an extra $3,000 in taxes, regardless of offsetting losses anywhere else on a tax return, says Bill Brennan. How? Take the difference between $40,000 and $20,000 and multiply it by 15%, and you get $3,000. Tax preferences can also affect adversely the 50% maximum tax computation, depending on your situation.

Perhaps the most critical blow the IRS can strike against the tax benefits of equipment leasing is in determining that a lease is actually a loan, says Brennan. In the past, the IRS has nixed the deductions on leasing transactions between closely affiliated groups by claiming that they were really loans by the user to the investor. That could happen in a situation, for example, where an investor bought a computer and leased it to a major company which in turn financed the investor's deal through its wholly owned finance subsidiary. While the IRS has issued specific guidelines, expert advice is still needed. "This is a complicated area without ready-made answers," notes Brennan.

To top it all, the IRS is quietly stalking the at-risk aspects of equipment lease financing, especially now that so many deals are coming out of brokerage firms, threatening to make equipment leasing rampantly popular. The spoilers in Washington seem to consider leasing transactions where only an act of God could put the kibosh on the user as decidedly less than risky.

In other words, leasing computers to General Motors for five years may not be deemed a risky investment even though the investor is personally on the hook to the finance company for the payments on the computer. GM is on the hook, too, and unless it goes down the tubes in five years, where's the risk?, the IRS may ask. This attitude goes right to the heart of tax shelter philosophy as originally designed by Congress: Risk generates write-off.

Of course, we all thought Chrysler was pretty solid at one time.

If your knuckles haven't turned white by now, there are some very good equipment leasing opportunities available. Action in railroad cars has chugged along swiftly in the past few years, according to Bob Underwood, who runs a financial planning firm under his name in Birmingham, Alabama. Underwood was one of the first advisors around to spot the potential of railroad cars a few years back, and has made equipment leasing one of his specialties. He's also hinted for several years that he'd like to see similar deals in shrimp boat leasing, but hasn't seen any economically sound deals as yet in that field.

As for railroad cars, there has been a shortage of this equipment, especially newer cars with safety devices. Although the rush into railroad boxcars in the past few years has resulted in a virtual glut on the market, there are still opportunities for closed hopper cars in the business of railroading—an industry which is vital to the national economy, as periodic strikes attest.

It's fairly easy to get a fix on the income one can expect in such a deal because the rates per mile are mandated by the Interstate Commerce Commission. Underwood points out, however, that those rates and the benefits of railroad car ownership apply only to major carriers—called Class One railroads.

Railroad leasing deals avoid practically all the tax pitfalls of other kinds of equipment leasing. For one thing, individuals, or sole proprietorships, are usually the owners of the cars, not limited partnerships. This can open up the way for the investment tax credit, since leases are generally written for two or three years, which is far less than half the 10 to 15-year useful life of a railroad car. What's more, operating expenses, such as management fees and maintenance costs, usually run between 16% and 25% of the annual revenues. In many cases, the management fee is structured in a way that helps meet this, the 15% rule, referred to earlier in this chapter.

In a typical deal, the investor turns the management of the car over to an independent company which receives a fee, and pays the maintenance costs out of the cash flow. After three or four years, when the accelerated depreciation starts falling off dramatically, an investor should still be able to get an 8% to 10% net-after-tax return on investment.

A typical railroad car costs between $30,000 and $50,000, and should be purchased new, says Underwood. That's because you can get all the depreciation, plus a bonus payment per mile from the ICC for types of cars where a shortage in the industry exists, especially those with all the new safety features. New cars are also easier to finance.

Many banks are willing to lend up to 80% on a new car. That kind of leverage plus depreciation can give between a 100% and 120% write-off the first year. And some promoters claim up to 150% write-off can be achieved—but most fail to mention the 15% minimum tax such a deal might trigger. Generally, any write-off over 120% may indicate too high a finance charge, and too little return on investment.

The deal is not without its risks. Your car might not be used on a regular basis, which would leave you on the hook for the loan you took out to finance the purchase. This has happened to many investors in boxcars recently. Second, there's always the possibility that your car will be involved in a disastrous accident. If that happened, you might be liable for the damage to the car itself as well as any damages caused by the car and its contents. A small sum, however, will buy a "mandated" insurance policy that will cover up to $25 million of damages for each car you own and lease. Besides, a good management company will arrange leases to carry chickens or cabbage rather than explosives or toxic chemicals.

There is a pitfall along the tracks, however: selling the railcars after you've ridden the depreciation into the ground. First, there's a very limited after-market for these cars when they're worn and grey. Second, the sale could well subject you to depreciation recapture problems—which means being hit with a surprise tax bill at 70% ordinary income, not 28% capital gains, rates. "We advise folks never to sell the car," says Underwood. To whom could you sell it? Railroads lease the latest equipment, and individuals need the tax benefits from a new in-use car. Hence, Underwood advises turning the property over to heirs, relatives, or charitable institutions which can continue to benefit from the rental income without worrying about the tax considerations. This brings in some very creative estate-planning and charitable contribution ploys when the equipment is paid off.

Then again, one could always put the car out to pasture, literally, and turn it into a restaurant—or single occupancy motel.

Part Seven

Exotica And Esoteric: Things That Go Bump In The Checkbook

21.

Far Out...
But Viable

You remember Exotica, don't you? She's that delightful investment advisor who pulls a whole assortment of dazzling baubles out of her portfolio purse for you to drool over ... items such as gold bars and certificates; diamonds and pearls; lithos by Miro and meticulous Monets; and, of course, bags of silver coins and commodity straddles. She's a foxy lady, this Exotica, especially when it comes to parading her tax shelter wares before your eyes. Her spiel is cool, languid, beguiling; she talks of tax breaks, soaring premiums for rare gems, metals, artworks. Trouble is, she's not very practical when it comes to protecting her clients, for they sometimes wind up with a case of *clapis leatheritis,* which is a particularly nasty form of venereal disease of the wallet.

(To avoid charges of sexism, let it be said that Exotica travels with a male companion—Esoteric—who sends visions of blissful and ecstatic tax evasion through the minds of high tax bracket women with his briefcase full of financial unguents and jewels. He's the kind of person you spot late at night in piano bars urging the musician at hand to tinkle out a chorus of "Just a Gigolo.")

The firm of Exotica & Esoteric are never at a loss to come up with tax-shelter schemes of the most outrageous kind. Sometimes lightning strikes, and they offer deals which actually have an economic purpose, but these are usually given short shrift by the partners because they are difficult to explain to potential clients, and lack the charisma of zapping Uncle Sam with concepts which make for good cocktail party chatter.

In this, our last section, we will deal with the tax-shelter schemes which require a true gambler's instinct, and either a sense of humor or sense of the absurd. This particular chapter will deal briefly with those tax shelters which appear to have some economic merit, far out though they may be in concept. The final chapter of this book will deal with those deals which make a Ponzi proud.

Federal Oil & Gas Leasing. This is one of the strangest crapshoots around, where the odds of making a decent return on your investment are so bad that it makes blackjack at a casino where the house can exclude the "counters" look like a good deal. However, it's a relatively cheap way of losing money—there's no leverage to worry about and the potential payoff is so great that the game annually attracts players ranging from the most sophisticated investment bankers to maw and paw on the ranch. The tax situation is absolutely clear: write-offs usually amount to 100% of the money put into the deal, and there are few pitfalls along the way.

Federal oil and gas leases are awarded to winners of a bi-monthly lottery conducted by the Bureau of Land Management, Department of the Interior. What you win is the right to lease oil and gas rights on federally owned land. The leases, which cost $1 per acre per year, are for parcels of between 40 and 2,560 acres. You can file only one bid for each lease, but note that each member of a family is considered a separate applicant. Large broods can try to tie up drilling rights to the isle of Manhattan, for example.

The idea is to win rights to a lease which might be re-leased (or, sold) to an oil company that's interested in exploring for oil and gas. If the company is interested in your lease, you can sell it at a profit and possibly get a share of the oil and gas revenues (royalty) if the driller scores a hit. An oil company may pay between $3 and $100 an acre to lease drilling rights from you. How much will depend upon the number of acres involved, the location of the field, and geological surveys, according to Stewart Capital Corporation, a New York firm which runs a lease-bidding service.

At best, only one in three leases are eventually re-leased to an oil company. Obviously, some parcels are geologically more promising than others, and if you win a lease, you should get a handle on what you might expect if you hire an experienced oil landman in the area to help appraise the parcel. (Ask for the recommendations of local banks.)

There are a number of pooling services, each with its own *modus operandi*. Stewart's program, which is called Devex, limits the number of subscribers to its service, and bids only on leases which it thinks will attract less than a certain number of bids, which will increase the probability of its clients winning. You can generally limit your cash exposure through a service like Devex by choosing to bid on a monthly basis, with no obligation to continue past that particular month. The cost of these services ranges from $150 to $995 per month, depending on the number of leases you wish to bid upon. This works out to more per bid than you'd actually pay if you submitted your name to the Bureau of Land Management yourself, but these lease-bidding services also include fees for computer time, analysis of land prospects, and references to landmen.

This is a big, but quiet, business. While the bulk of federal lands can be considered nonproducing or marginal prospects, there has been increased domestic drilling of late to take advantage of the higher prices for oil and gas. The government makes a tidy sum on this lottery each year, and some people who bid on leases have been known to experience delightful windfalls. One never can tell what might lie beneath federal property in Manhattan.

Magazines, Newsletters. Exotica and Esoteric refer to these deals as "subscription shelters," and they can be the sexiest of all the legitimate far-out deals. That's because the magazine and newsletter businesses are booming, for several reasons. We are in an age of specialization, where the consumer is willing to pay for information related directly to his or her own needs. Thus, the proliferation of magazines ranging from *Self* to *Venture,* from *Working Woman* to *Blueboy,* from *Firehouse* to *Wet,* the latter of which is all about new and exciting ways to bathe, and is very big in certain parts of California.

Newsletters on every conceivable investment topic, plus those which deal with government regulatory actions and politics, have cropped up of late—many of which command outrageously high subscription prices from a growing list of clientele. The high subscription costs in newsletters make them more of an economic deal in the short run compared to magazines, which traditionally take up to three years to get in the black. That's because magazines are dependent upon advertising revenue for profits, and advertisers generally like to wait around for a while before committing dollars to new publications. Still, the high cost of television advertising has prompted many advertisers to place cheaper ad schedules in new magazines sooner, and this has helped the cash flow situation somewhat.

I've been involved in the start-up of half a dozen magazines from several points of view—as publisher, editor, or contributor. In every case, the story is the same: magazines are cash-eaters which cannot survive on subscription income at all. In fact, technically, this income cannot be used as it comes in, but only as each monthly issue is published on a pro rata basis. Thus, if a magazine has $1 million in revenues from 100,000 subscribers, only 1/12th—or $83,000—of that amount can be used each month to pay for the costs of producing that magazine—printing, paper, staff, photography, color separations, overhead, writers. Since printing costs alone can amount to $75,000 per month in a situation like that, you can see how dependent magazines are on advertising, and why so much money has to be raised for even the most modest of publications. It can take up to $4 million to get a national magazine with a circulation of 100,000 off the ground—and that's *before* you start seeing a return on investment. When it comes, however, the return can be very big, indeed, and part of the reason lies in the charm of the subscription tax shelter.

When you invest in a subscription shelter, you are paying money to acquire subscribers. That means you are paying for the costs of acquiring and using direct mail lists, printing millions of subscription letters (commonly known as "junk mail"), postage, return postage, advertising agency fees, etc. You are under a federal obligation (Federal Trade Commission) to *deliver* each copy of the magazine you promise in that direct mail

campaign and, as such, the IRS has determined that you
are under a *recourse loan* obligation to the subscribers.
A-ha! you say, here we go again, personal liability. Yes,
and that's the reason you can't technically spend the
subscription money in advance (although, truth to tell,
every publisher I've ever met does; magazines require
large doses of daily cash for the oddest, and most insane,
reasons).

In addition to the up-front costs of direct mail (which
are fully deductible, one dollar for one dollar, a 100%
write-off), you are also able to deduct the cost of *fulfill-
ment*—or the physical delivery of each issue of the
subscription term—in advance. Thus, the costs of maintaining subscriber lists and postage for each of the
issues covered by the subscription can be deducted in
advance since you are under a recourse obligation to
deliver those copies. Hence, you can boost your tax
shelter substantially without additional cash outlays by
going in debt, theoretically, to your subscribers.

But, you'd better deliver.

Subscription shelters are one of the few where it actually pays to go into the deal at the end of the year.
That's because you can write off all the costs in one year
without putting the income from the direct mail effort on
the books until the next year. There's also a very sound
business reason for this tactic: The end of the year is one
of the best times to seek business through the mail according to all the direct mail experts. Returns are somehow higher around the holidays than at most other
times. Just check the amount of junk mail in your
mailbox around that time, and you'll agree.

Needless to say, a subscription shelter is one which
should not be considered at the end of the year unless
you've had several months of discussion about the concept of the magazine in advance with both the entre-

preneurs involved and your tax advisors. You must be absolutely committed to publishing, and to the concept of the magazine, to be the kind of cat who goes into these deals. If you're just looking for a tax shelter, and haven't got the psychological staying power needed to see the publication through its early stages, you would be much better off feeding cattle, or drilling for oil in Rockefeller Center.

R & D. We seem to be in a new age of entrepreneurialism, with much of the activity for new business ventures centering around technological innovation. These are high-risk, management-intensive ventures which require sophisticated investment packages, usually put together by venture capital firms staffed with some of the best brains to come out of Cambridge, Palo Alto, New York, and Philadelphia—the Harvard/Stanford/Wall Street/Wharton cabal.

Because high-technology deals are so risky, these deals have been limited in the past to those who can truly afford the crapshoots involved. They are the ones my investment banking friend Barry Bloomfield likes to call the cats who are looking for "the new Xeroxes"—companies where they can take an equity position for relatively few dollars, and then sell out on a public market for big bucks.

But the demand for capital, and the need for tax shelter on the part of more people, has led to a hybrid venture capital deal called the "R & D Shelter," short for research and development. Lots of these deals are coming out of the woodwork, notably under the auspices of Wall Street firms. If you're approached by your broker, you may want to take a close look at the way things are structured, and to spend some investigative time checking up not only on the technology involved, but its marketability as well. There are many solid technological improvements which engineers and scientists dream up in their basements which have absolutely no chance of succeeding on the open market either because the market doesn't understand the technology involved, or they are slightly ahead of their time.

Basically, an R & D shelter is an investment in the incubation stages. You pay for the costs of maintaining an entrepreneurial team for a certain period of time, during which they promise to refine a concept and produce a marketable prototype of the product or system in question. You generally get a 100% write-off of your investment, in return for either a royalty on the sales of the products involved, or conversion of your limited partnership interests into equity some time in the future.

There are rare possibilities for leverage in R & D deals, since investors would be very reluctant to become at-risk for products or ideas with little or no prior history. And entrepreneurs are usually not the kind who have the wherewithal to guarantee letters of credit or other types of leverage.

There are a host of other ways these deals can be structured, but keep in mind that since you probably can't get better than a 100% write-off going in, you'll want a deal which will maximize the future income you'll receive if the research develops into the new Xerox or Pet Rock. Therefore, pay close attention to the conditions for payout. If you are to be paid a royalty, never settle for a fixed-dollar amount, because if inflation continues to gallop along, your actual rate-of-return may be lower than you expected. Go for a royalty based on a fixed percentage of sales prices; depending on the product involved, you might wind up with enough income in the future to keep rolling your receipts over into other shelters, which is a situation we should all have.

Straddles. One of the things which bothers me about the world of finance is that the more complicated and

sophisticated an investment strategy, the more people
are attracted to it who haven't got the foggiest idea of
how to balance their own checkbooks. Such is the case in
straddles, a ploy which involves either commodities or
financial instruments traded on a variety of exchanges
throughout the world.

Listen, if you don't understand the way the commodity or financial futures contracts business works,
then either learn about it, or avoid it completely. In these
deals, you're hedging your bets by simultaneously buying and selling contracts in the same commodities
(wheat, frozen pork bellies, corn, silver) or financial instruments (Treasury Bills). You do this late enough in
the year so that you can close out (sell) the losing contract (the one which turns out to be the wrong bet, or the
wrong side of the straddle), in order to take a big loss in
that particular year. Then, you wait until after everyone
sings "Auld Lang Syne" and take your profits on the
winning contract. In the case of commodity futures (including T-Bills), your waiting period for capital gains tax
treatment on the winning end is only six months, not the
full year involved in all other kinds of transactions.

Straddles, especially in T-Bills, have become so
popular of late that the IRS has asked Congress to intro-
duce legislation which would severely crimp the attraction of these shelters. How? Well, ask yourself the question: How can I lose if I'm playing both sides against the
middle by simultaneously going "long" and "short" in
the same commodity? You really can't, because your loss
is going to be wiped out by your gain, since your contracts are due to expire at the same time.

The IRS would like you to wait 30 days between
buying and selling before you can take the loss you hope
for. Since the fluctuations of the commodities and financial futures markets are such that whole fortunes can be

wiped out overnight, one can rest assured that should legislation come to pass regarding this tax shelter, you won't hear too much about straddles in the future—unless you're a gynecologist.

22.

Praise The Lord
—And Pass The
Tax Deduction

It's been very difficult to approach this chapter with a
straight face, since we will now deal with some of the
more outrageous examples of tax shelters on the market
these days. In the interests of fair journalism, however—
and the hopes that most readers will take this chapter
seriously—I have studiously avoided imbibing in, or in-
haling, any foreign substance which would play tricks
with my imagination. Besides, we're about to touch upon
a subject which many people consider very serious indeed, the Bible. We will also discuss tax shelters in
master works and mining in this chapter, which means
the heading at the top of this page could have read,
"Bibles, Breughels, and Beads," rather than the sacri-
lege which is set in type.

Please understand. I have nothing against the Bible. In fact, I'm pretty much in favor of religion as a whole. But alas and alack, I have also read my share of history, and have come to discover that every time religion gets mixed up with economics, the result is a situation which would make Christ, Mohammed, Moses, and Buddha seriously consider banding together to create a worldwide pox, so as to start all over again.

Look what happened to Alexander the Great's empire when the high priests got their hands on the money. There's been a long line of Popes, especially the Borgias, whose rather unsubtle handling of indulgences and other kinds of salvation led to a few other major historical dislocations in addition to the Reformation. And we all know what happened when the mullahs took over Iran.

If God had intended religion and economics to mix, he would have allowed Cosimo de' Medici to start his own religion, The Holy Rollers, and we'd all be *paying* to receive communion or be *bar mitzvahed* by now.

That's basically why I find this particular business about bibles and tax shelters to be a bit of a cynical trap dreamed up by slick promoters with countenances which literally *beam* with glory in order to play on the two most universal emotions of mankind—greed and the fear of the Lord. I have seen two twists on this game, which come out of two other basic types of tax-shelter "industries." The first was an attempt to structure a deal involving bibles written in 11th-century Armenian as an investment in a "master work." The second type of bible deal floating around these days is grounded in the old "charitable contribution" racket. Both were big hits with both sophisticated and bubbleheaded investors, both are sold in the face of dire warnings and IRS rulings about their legitimacy and, to my mind, both come pretty close to bordering on fraud.

That's as far as my publisher will allow me to go.

Thus, this discussion on The Bible Game (sounds like a new daytime television game show) will also look at the twists and turns in master works of all kinds, and various kinds of charitable contribution programs.

In the master work deal involving bible production and sales which came to my attention, the attraction was a write-off which exceeded five times the cash investment. On every single common sense count of investment (let alone, tax shelter) viability, this particular concept failed to make even the slightest dent as to credibility. The frightening thing about it, however, was the fact that the person who showed me the deal had been handed the prospectus by his *accountant* as something to "consider" after he discovered in November that his client was going to have a pretty big tax bill. This entire episode which I shall now detail offers a perfect insight into the kinds of people who make absolutely perfect targets for unscrupulous or cynical promoters—people like you and me.

George was an executive with a major firm, responsible for some areas which touched on real estate. He'd been transferred cross-country the previous year by his company, and his expenses had been picked up, mostly in the form of a deferred bonus for tax purposes. George knew that he'd be faced with some kind of tax problem at least a year in advance of the Ides of April, and knew that he should do something about it. His wife also worked, and they rented, did not own, property. George and his wife were not doing badly, and were planning to buy a co-op in real estate mad Manhattan, but needed more cash for a good down payment. He talked with his accountant about it in April (of course), and left him with a request to hunt up a suitable strategy based on what the accountant projected as a tax liability.

In October, the accountant called back. George's response should have been to shoot his accountant for taking five months to get back to him, but George felt guilty because he hadn't really pressed the issue.

In any case, the accountant told George that he was facing a tax bill of around $10,000 more than he'd been used to paying, and that it was pretty late in the year to start planning to reduce that bill. But, there was a way of trying to wipe out that liability, and maybe qualify for a refund to boot.

It was a tax shelter, and, "Here, why don't you take a look." Nothing about the deal was explained to George, who took the prospectus home and tried to make sense of it. Somehow, he wound up plopping it on my desk, via an intermediary, for an interpretation.

By page 11 I was doubled up in hysteria. First of all, let me tell you that George is a nice Jewish boy from New Jersey who should have known something was strange when he looked at the name of the venture on the front page of the prospectus: Massada [*sic*]. If I recall, Masada was the site of a mass suicide by the Jews, who vowed never to live under Roman rule. This, I thought, is a parody. But these guys were *serious*.

They proposed to print and distribute copies of rare bibles written in 11th century Armenia for the then king of the land. My first question was, of course, "Did Armenia *exist* in the 11th century? And, by the way, where *is* Armenia?" These bibles, it turns out, had been recently discovered, I believe, in some shrine in Jerusalem, where they'd no doubt been gathering dust through an assortment of religious and political crusades in the area.

The purpose of the deal was to make beautiful copies of these bibles, and sell the limited editions to a number of investors who were looking for a tax shelter. The investors would be able to act as distributors of these bibles, and sell them for many hundreds of dollars apiece, because they were rare limited editions of "literary property." In return, the investors would get the 10% investment tax credit, and accelerated depreciation on the value of the plates—which, you can be assured, was a high number. In addition, the deal was heavily leveraged, with notes all over the place, ostensibly on a *recourse* basis.

George was being asked to take delivery of a couple of hundred rare limited editions of a bible written in 11th century Armenia and sell them to anyone he could convince it was in their interests to buy.

I asked George if he had any idea what this deal was all about. After a sufficiently blank stare, he admitted that it had something to do with bibles. I then asked him if he'd seen the movie, *Paper Moon*, with Ryan O'Neal and his kid, Tatum. That's the one about the traveling bible salesman and his con-girl kid. He began to get my point.

First of all, this deal was being marketed out of a foreign country, by a company which looked like it could have been set up by an American on the lam. I had once seen a hilarious deal marketed out of Scandinavia for toy molds (depreciation on plastic elephants, very sexy) by some failed stockbroker from the Bronx, and this one seemed to fit the mold, so to speak. Talk about trying to meet the promoters! You've got to *find* them first.

Then we had the price of the "plates" and rights to the works: somewhere around $15,000 cash, *plus* a nonrecourse $92,000 note which brought the value of the bible limited editions to $107,000. So, we were going to base our investment tax credit and depreciation on that figure. Never mind that the IRS was in the business of

examining whether such distribution agreements consti-
tuted a lease and, therefore, no tax advantages could be
claimed. What about the *fair market value* of these
books? And, were they books—or were they works of
art? Here we run into other possible tax problems. Books
are considered depreciable items by the IRS, by virtue of
their copyright, and "tangible" character; but some so-
called "tangible properties" involving master plates (or,
in the case of movies, negatives) are not considered very
tangible at all by the Service. Were these bibles books
(you can't copyright the apostles), or works of art? This
deal was fraught with an identity crisis, as well as all
sorts of tax and financial pitfalls.

George did not go into this deal. Instead, he fired his
accountant, gave a goodly sum to his alma mater, took a
charitable deduction, and paid some taxes, too. I don't
know whether any investors bought into the deal, but if
someone comes knocking on your door trying to sell you
bibles in Armenian at discount, let me know.

The trouble with any tax shelter which is involved
with master plates is that the fair market value of the
products in question are almost invariably overstated by
the promoters. Deals which involve original lithographs
commissioned from famous contemporary artists are
just another example of this kind of appeal to the
Cosimo de' Medici in all of us. The IRS has attacked
these deals on several fronts, but seems to have come up
with the jugular on the fair market value argument.
They simply went out and hired independent art appraisers to come up with the right figures in one particular art deal and, lo and behold, guess who took it in
the neck? Not the promoter, who pocketed all sorts of
fees on the deal, you can be sure. The people who are invariably recaptured during the auditing process of a
master work tax shelter are the investors. These deals
are being monitored in Washington, and the IRS is

quietly assembling a number of panels of experts to help build their case against these deals.

Beware!

The other bible deal involves this current mania to donate appreciated property held for a year to charitable institutions. In this kind of a deal, a promoter sells something of value to an investor, usually at a *discount* from the retail, or fair market, value. The investor then holds the item—gems, art, antiques, plants (yes, plants), or books—for more than a year, and then donates it to various institutions and takes a tax deduction based on the full retail or "fair market" value. So, if you buy bibles for say, $10 apiece, and they retail for $30, you write off the $30. Neat, hah? Just think of all the bibles you can give away in your own neighborhood, folks. Except for one little problem, which naturally leads to another. The IRS issued a ruling in late 1980 which was designed to put a whammy on this kind of shelter, but that apparently did not stop some promoters from adding new wrinkles. The IRS issued another adverse ruling, but according to newsletter publisher Bill Brennan, this deal is still widely advertised. "It seems preposterous that anyone could seriously consider (this deal) plausible," Brennan comments.

Bibles, even if written in Armenian, don't cost that much to produce, and they don't command such a high retail ticket. Ergo, you have to buy a *lot* of bibles in order to qualify for a fairly hefty deduction if you're in the 50% tax bracket. The IRS may take note of this, and claim that you're actually a dealer in bibles, and are unqualified to take the deductions on charitable grounds; or, they simply may declare the deal a sham based on the genuine economic factors involved—which seem very nonexistent, indeed. Phil Strassler of the CPA firm of Kenneth Leventhal & Company, who noted this kind of stuff was going over big in southern California of late, opined that there would soon be so many bible-dealing tax-shelter holy rollers that there'd soon be bible drive-in facilities dotting the highways of Orange and Los Angeles counties. Just drive up and get your charitable contribution.

Look, we've had some fun here, but I've meant to be serious about two things: Be very careful about deals involving master works; they are under active attack from the IRS and don't look all that economically viable either. Second, as general investment advice, be wary of someone who tries to mix religion and money.

To end on a lighter note, we turn to beads. Specifically, precious gems and the mining thereof. If you recall in our remarks about coal, most mining deals involve the payment of advance royalties in the form of cash and notes to a landowner for the right to mine. The payoff in gems, of course, is that their price is rising faster than coal. *If* they're gems.

Most of these deals are marketed out of South America. They involve emeralds, opals, and other precious and semi-precious stones. Aside from the fact that deals out of South America usually last as long as governments on that continent, one should ask a question about the motivation of a promoter who would want to give up the rights to those rapidly appreciating pieces of rock. Either the promoter's not too bright, or there are no stones there.

Which brings us down to the basics of tax shelter investing in the 1980s. You are dealing with *your* money, and you should take all precautions to preserve as much of it as you can from the long arm of the law, and the quick fingers of the promoter. That means any deal you look at, any deal you hear about, should be able to pass a stringent test of investment criteria before you even consider the tax angles. Then, you should make sure the tax strategy is not only sound, but also compatible with your personal financial goals and portfolio. If the deal passes muster, and you have the temperament to live with the kinds of disasters which can and do occur in each of the tax-shelter industries we've discussed, then you should make up your mind whether to write a check or pay the tax.

In summation, a tax shelter is only as good as the investment potential behind it. Or, as the farmer's wife says, "Pigs is pigs."

Epilogue

The Ten Commandments
Of Tax Shelters

1. *Thou shalt not invest in a locker room deal.* This can lead to athlete's wallet.

2. *Thou shalt listen to thy common sense.* If it doesn't make sense to you, how about the IRS?

3. *Thou shalt trust thy CPA's opinion.* But only if he or she doesn't suggest a particular deal to you.

4. *Thou shalt ask thy spouse.* Or, if single, thy lawyer; same difference.

5. *Thou shalt not bite off more than the IRS alloweth you to chew.* Be careful of high leverage; you can get goosed.

6. *Thou shalt not expose thy assets to recourse notes.*

7. *Thou shalt not be shy.* Meet the promoters, damn it.

8. *Thou shalt not covet thy neighbor's write-offs.* Never go for deduction over economic benefit.

9. *Thou shalt not be a December bridesmaid.* Invest in the beginning of the year to get the best deals.

10. *To tax is human; to escape all consequences belongs strictly to the Divine.*

Index

Accelerated depreciation, 115
  equipment leasing and, 198
  farming and, 166
  in real estate syndicates, 100-101
  recapture and, 118-119
Accounting
  See Certified Public Accountant
American College, 23
Apartments, as tax shelters, 103-108
Audits, Internal Revenue Service and, 81-87

Back-auditing, 48
Balanced program, oil well drilling and, 151
Bibles, 216, 217-222
Blind-pool income syndicates, 99-100
Blind-pool tax shelter, 100
Breeding
  See Horse racing; Cattle feeding
Brennan Reports, 59
Bureau of Land Management, federal oil and gas leases and, 207, 208

Capital gains, Tax Reform Act of 1969 and, 67-68
Cattle feeding, 162, 183-184
  dairy farming and, 187-191
  depreciation, 166
  economics of, 185-186, 187
  financing, 184
  profits and, 163
  timing of investment, 184, 186-187
Certified Financial Planner (CFP), 23-28
Certified Public Accountant (CPA), 18-23, 28
CFP (Certified Financial Planner), 23-28
Charitable contributions, 16, 217
  IRS Bulletin and, 82
  master work donation as, 221
Chartered Life Underwriters (CLU), 24
Coal tax shelters, 132, 134, 137-141
College for Financial Planning, 23
Commercial property, 121-127
Commission

  of financial planners, 26-27
  promoters and, 76
Commodity future contracts, 212-214
Completion program, oil well drilling and, 151-152
Computers, tax return processed by, 21
Conflict-of-interest
  in real estate syndicates, 99
  promoters and, 77-78
Cows, dairy farming and, 187-191
  See also Cattle feeding

Dairy farming, 187-191
Department of Agriculture, Farm Home Loan Bank program, 119-120
Department of Housing and Urban Development (HUD), Section 8 housing and, 109-120
Development wells, 151

Economic Recovery Tax Act (ERTA), 3-5, 10
  horse racing and, 175
  real estate and, 92
  tax rate schedules and, 12
Energy tax shelters, 131-132
  coal, 132, 134-135, 137-141
  See also Oil/gas tax shelters
Equipment leasing, 195-196
  accelerating depreciation and, 198
  establishing, 196-197
  investment tax credit and, 197-198
  as loan, 199
  problems in, 197-198
  railroad cars, 199-202
  reasons for, 197
Esoterica, 205-206
  fair market values and, 45-49
  federal oil and gas leasing, 206-208
  magazines and newsletters, 208-211
  research and development (R and D), 211-212
  straddles, 212-214
Exotica
  See Esoterica
Exploratory wells, 151
Extradition, 79

MSFS (Master of Science in Financial
  Services), 23-24

Negative taxable income, 44
Newsletters, 58, 208-211

Office buildings, 122, 123, 125
  commercial property, 121-127
Oil and gas leasing, federal, 206-208
Oil/gas tax shelters, 57, 64, 132, 143
  assessments, 156
  benefits, 134, 135
  deductions from, 144-146
  drilling programs, 151-152
  evaluation, 143-144, 149-150
  financial arrangements, 154-155
  growth of, 133-134
  letter of credit and, 145-146
  liquidity, 155, 157
  past performance, 156-157
  people involved in, 153
  prospectus examination, 152-157
  public tax shelters and, 152
  risk of, 150
  structure of, 153-154
  tax savings from, 147-148
  wells drilled, 151

Partnerships, in tax shelters, 31-34,
  42
  See also Limited partnerships
Payout on a program basis, 154
Payout on a well-to-well basis, 154
Personal Financial Planner, 22-28
Planning, 15-17
  decisions, 41-42
  financial, 22-28
  See also Financial advisor
Private Placement Memorandum, 31
Private tax shelters, 27, 63-65
  in coal, 137
  factors to beware of, 79
  in real estate, 96, 97
Promoters, 32, 68-69, 85
  conflict-of-interest and, 77-78
  credit of, 74
  criteria for choosing, 74-80
  factors to beware of, 78-80
  fee schedules, 76-77
  finances of, 75-76
  meeting promoter, 73-74
  nature of, 71-72
  oil/gas shelters and, 153-154
  reason for, 69-71
  spread, 78
  staff qualifications, 75
  Tax Reform Act of 1969 and, 67-68
Prospectus, 31

information from, 60
  oil/gas tax shelters and, 152-157
  of real estate syndicate, 99
Public tax shelters, 27, 61-62, 63
  oil/gas shelters and, 152
  in real estate, 97

Racing
  See Horse racing
Railroad cars, investing in, 197-202
  See also Equipment leasing
Real estate, 44, 91, 92
  apartments, 103-108
  commercial property, 121-128
  Department of Housing and Urban
    Development projects, 109-120
  depreciation, 100-101
  factors to beware of, 94-96, 97-98,
    99-101
  optimum approach, 98-99
  popularity of, 92-93
  promoter fees, 76
  syndicates in, 93-98, 99-101
  wraparound mortgage, 97-98
Recapture, 45, 118-119
  federal housing project and, 118-
    119
  Recording industry, fair market
    value and, 46-47, 48
Recourse loan obligation, 210
Research and development (R and D),
  211-212
Revenue Act of 1978, 3
  leverage and, 44
  real estate and, 92
Risk, 16, 30, 34, 39
  leverage and, 44-45
  real estate and, 92

Section 8, HUD and, 109-120
Securities and Exchange Commis-
  sion, public tax shelters and, 61-62
Seminars, on tax shelters, 58-59
Shopping centers, 121, 122, 125, 126
  commercial property, 121-128
Society of Independent Financial
  Advisors (SIFA), 27
Spread, 78
Stanger Report, The, 59, 145
Straddles, 212-215
Straight-line depreciation, 101
  recapture and, 118
Subscription shelters, 208-211
Syndicates, 31-32, 33-34
  in real estate, 93-98, 99-101

Tax advisor, 13
Tax attorney, 18